POLICE HANDGUN MANUAL

POLICE HANDGUN MANUAL

How to Get Street-Smart Survival Habits

Bill Clede

*Photos by Author
unless otherwise credited*

Stackpole Books

Library of Congress Cataloging in Publication Data

Clede, Bill.
    Police handgun manual.

    1. Police—Equipment and supplies.   2. Pistol shooting.
I. Title.
HV7936.E7C53   1985   683.4'3'0243632   84-16161
ISBN 0-8117-1275-3

Contents

Acknowledgments

No book is ever the product of only one man's motivation and knowledge. There are many who contribute. I go back to when Air Force Sgt. Pat Barnes coached the University of Maryland rifle team and me to a National Championship in 1950; and when Stanley A. Mate joined the National Rifle Association in 1954 to head up the then-new Training Section. He was a professional trainer, who broke the mold when it came to explaining the "science" of shooting. Charles L. Smith, a former FBI firearms instructor who established the Smith & Wesson Academy in 1970, recognized the need to update what was then being taught to policemen and founded the International Association of Law Enforcement Firearms Instructors. Robert E. Hunt, former Lt. Col., Massachusetts State Police turned traditional training courses at the S&W Academy into modern challenges and gave me a new insight into gun skill. Who better than Hunt to demonstrate various aspects of shooting in many of the photos. Bill Vanderpool of the Firearms Training Unit at the FBI Academy read and corrected the preliminary manuscript for this book. Many others, too numerous to mention, met the challenge, became proficient shooters, and were of great assistance to me.

Why This Book and
Why This Writer?

You can't learn to shoot by reading a book. Physical skills that require eye-hand coordination must be tried, practiced, and experienced in a physical way in order to be learned. It's more a matter of developing good motor habits than of gaining mental knowledge. This is also true of driving a car and flying an airplane.

While physical skills must be developed rather than learned, understanding the whys and wherefores first can make skill development easier.

My first introduction to guns was from a gun collector friend in Oklahoma City. My first formal training in shooting was at the Augusta Military Academy in Virginia. During World War II, the U.S. Navy provided the usual boot camp sessions on the firing range. After the war, I went to college. To help feed a young family on the GI Bill payments, I served as a patrolman on the Edmonston (Maryland) Police Department. Firearms training then was virtually non-existent, so the Municipal Police Association of Prince Georges County sponsored a basic pistol course at the University of Maryland range. It was a first experience for many of the police officers who took the course.

You've heard the "horror story" of an officer showing up for training with a gun in such poor condition he couldn't get his cylinder open? It actually happened in that class. His gun had been so neglected that the cartridges had corroded in its cylinder. A wooden mallet finally broke it free, and it took a good half hour to get his revolver clean enough to shoot.

The college rifle team was the real challenge. We had great coaches and no less than two Olympic shooters on the team. I thought scoring 285 out of a possible 300 was doing rather poorly. It's like the bumble bee story. When his helicopter was criticized, Igor Sikorsky would retort, "Aerodynamically, the bumble bee is incapable of flight. But he's too stupid to know that, so he goes ahead and flies anyway."

My learning to fly was a different experience. It's learned like shooting, one-on-one. You and the instructor are up there alone. It seemed such a mystery. When you pull back on the stick, the nose points up and you climb. Right? When you open the throttle, the engine runs faster and you speed up. That's logical. It was not until later that I came to understand that pulling back on the stick doesn't make you climb. It slows your speed. And opening the throttle doesn't make you go faster. It makes you climb.

This little spark of understanding was gleaned from a book, *Stick and Rudder* by Wolfgang Langeweische. Its subtitle was "An Explanation of the Art of Flying." Published in 1944, that book gave me an understanding of flight that made the practical lessons I received later comprehensible. I believe I am a better pilot today for having really understood what the instructor was talking about.

That's what I hope to accomplish with this book. When it comes to learning about guns and using them on the street, it is easier when you really understand *why* things happen the way they do.

In the mid-1950s, as a staff assistant with the National Rifle Association, I "won the honor" of revising and rewriting old texts for the NRA's expanding schedule of courses. All these texts were straight sermons, pontifications, with relatively few down-to-earth examples.

The challenges facing policemen today, however, are vastly different from what they were in the 1950s.

To explain my qualifications for writing a book like this, you should know that I am a part-time sworn police officer in Windsor, Connecticut. My full-time job is with an agency doing public relations work for Smith & Wesson. I am presently a certified Police Firearms Instructor (S&W Academy), a Handgun Retention Trainer (Justice System Training Association), a Kubotan Instructor (Defensive Tactics Institute), a charter member of the International Association of Law Enforcement Firearms Instructors, and a Life Member of the National Rifle Association. I held an NRA Training Counselor rating, which qualified me for teaching civilian firearms training instructors.

I've faced the problem on the range of a young recruit who hardly knew one end of a gun from the other. He reminded me of the mysteries in my learning to fly, and he showed me the need for a different kind of a book on shooting.

This book will not teach you how to shoot. But it will explain all you ever need to know to do it right. I hope it makes learning easier, by giving you an understanding of what makes good shooting and, more importantly, understanding the considerations and responsibilities that go along with using firearms as tools of your trade.

Bill Clede

1

Changing Your Ways
May Help

Far be it from me to complain about the way you shoot. But if you're not a Master Class shooter, the knowledge of recent changes in shooting techniques may help. If your firearms instructor went through the FBI National Academy prior to 1982, he's not up to date.

Special Agent Bill Vanderpool of the FBI Firearms Training Unit came from Quantico to the 1982 National Training Conference of the International Association of Law Enforcement Firearms Instructors at Annapolis Jct., Maryland, to tell us about how FBI training has changed. It's a lot different now than it used to be.

For example, it's a good bet that you learned to shoot point-shoulder, using the isosceles triangle stance – both arms straight, elbows locked. The FBI is now teaching the Weaver stance, named for Jack Weaver, a southern California police sergeant.

In the Weaver stance, you quarter the target, gun side away, and punch the shooting arm across your chest. The two-hand grip *pulls* with the weak hand, *pushes* with the strong. The weak arm is bent. You can even break your strong elbow and Magnum cartridge recoil will be more straight back than rising, according to the FBI videotape demonstration. In barricade shooting, if you use a two-hand grip and lay the back of the weak hand

Special Agent Bill Vanderpool of the FBI Academy Firearms Training Unit (Quantico, Virginia) instructs a student agent in the Weaver stance. *National Rifle Association Photo.*

against the barricade, you've already taken the Weaver stance. So, it's not a bit mysterious!

For years we've learned the old straight prone position. You know, the one that almost breaks your neck. True, it presents the least possible target to an assailant. But anyone who flops down in the middle of a parking lot, rather than diving for cover, is using poor tactics.

The FBI now teaches the roll-over prone position. The body is at an angle to the target — as if you're shooting around a tire, hillock, or some other cover. You probably are, and you wouldn't use a straight prone position under those circumstances. In the roll-over prone position, your shooting arm is straight and your cheek lays comfortably on your biceps. The weak arm is bent — sort of a Weaver stance, lying down. You can even cock the gun to the side to get under a low obstacle, if you need to.

The old hip shooting crouch position is no good if the subject is within grabbing distance. It's an open invitation to grab your gun. When you're interviewing someone, stand at an angle, gun side away from him. If he draws on you, you need to get a shot off — fast.

Bill Jordan, an ex-U.S. Border Patrol officer and author of *No Second Place Winner*, developed a different technique that offers two advantages. the FBI is now training its agents and visiting police officers in the Jordan *Close Combat* hip position. To respond to the attack while you're interviewing a subject, you step back with your strong foot. Your weak hand tosses whatever it is holding to distract the assailant as your strong hand comes down to the butt of your gun. You then simply rotate the gun up and out of the holster and leave it right at your side as you level it at the assailant and pull the trigger. What could be quicker? And your left arm can fend off the assailant. The gun is held in close to your body so that he can't take it away from you.

The agent's holster also is of a new design, a pancake-style that's cut away in front to make the Close Combat draw even quicker.

Back when I first wore a badge, I learned that the first quick shot may well hit the dirt in front of the target, but that marvelous computer in your head compensates with the rapid second shot which goes right in. With practice, your first shot should be right on target; the impact of the second hit multiplies the effects of the first.

The FBI is now teaching the "double tap." Bang. Bang. Always fire *twice* — when facing a single assailant.

Range procedures have already changed to eliminate some of the habits that make life easier on the range but get guys killed on the street. Since California's infamous Newhall incident (more on that later), we know that you have to practice with the loads you carry. If you can't handle Magnums, you're better off with .38 Special + P. You dump your brass on the ground and don't think about picking it up. You drop your speedloader. You can look for it *after* the target is no longer a threat.

Another range safety command is biting the dust: "Clear and holster an empty weapon." Tradition says that guns on the range must be unloaded, except when actually firing. But the most dangerous thing in the world to a police officer is an *unloaded* gun. Aside from accidents with "unloaded" guns, what happens if you holster an unloaded gun — as you were trained on the range — and the gunfight rekindles?

The FBI and many progressive police departments are now running *hot* ranges. After your last six-shot string, you immediately reload and bring the gun back up to just below eye level. Then you check your target and the ones to either side for a few seconds before you reholster the loaded gun. You may even have to "top off" the cylinder in the middle of a course by removing only the fired cases and replacing them with live rounds. On the street, your gun should *never* sit unloaded.

Much thought has gone into how police officers are being trained to respond with firearms and how dangerous habits can be avoided. Both shooting and teaching techniques are changing, and most firearms instructors need to go back to school for "updating" sessions.

2

Gunsmithing Is Not
a Do-It-Yourself Hobby

"A little knowledge can be a dangerous thing," the old saying goes. And that's especially true when it comes to your handgun.

Only a few shooters become so "smart" with their revolvers that they contract the target shooter syndrome: "I'll just smooth up the trigger a bit." "Maybe I can lighten the trigger pull." "I'm just *dying* to see what's under that sideplate."

That last comment could be prophetic if the man with the screwdriver is not only a gunsmith, but one experienced with the particular brand of revolver you carry. So, let me satisfy your curiosity before you start tinkering.

The inner workings of a modern revolver are complex. Metal parts link and work together in a precise sequence of events. If they don't, you could find yourself with an almost acceptable hammer when what you need is a gun.

As the trigger is pulled (double-action), the hammer is cocked, the cylinder rotates until it is engaged by the cylinder stop, which lines up the cartridge precisely with the bore of the barrel. Then the hammer block drops out of the way so that the final trigger travel releases the hammer from the cam of the trigger, allowing the firing pin to strike the primer of the cartridge.

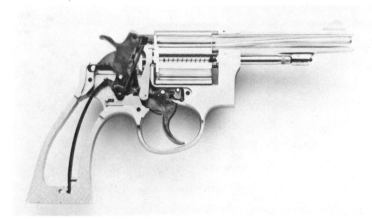

This cutaway view of a Model 10 revolver shows the intricate mechanism that must be in "time" to function properly. Work on your gun is best left to the deft hands of a qualified armorer. *Smith & Wesson Photo.*

As for your "improving the action," the result could be upsetting to this precision balance.

One officer I know "lightened" his trigger pull by grinding down the mainspring strain screw. He didn't know that he was lightening the hammer blow at the same time. Maybe, just maybe, the force of the hammer fall wouldn't be enough to ignite a hard primer when some joker pulls a gun on you.

The strain screw puts tension on the hammer spring of a revolver and should be snug and left alone. Relieving it either with a file or by backing it off could lead to a mechanical failure at the worst possible time.

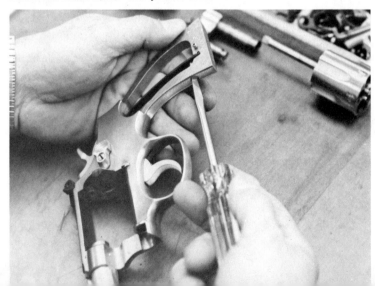

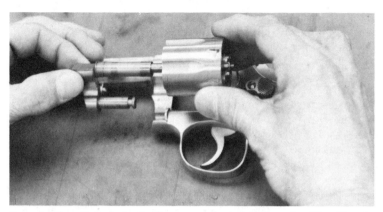

Removing the cylinder is simple, if you remember to hold it steady while pulling the yoke out of the frame. This procedure avoids scratches.

If the strain screw on your gun has been backed off (or shortened), screw it in tight (or replace it with a new one).

Nothing smoothes up the trigger pull better than using it. Like an automobile, a new piece of machinery needs to be "broken in." Practice on the target range "works in" both shooter and sidearm. If it doesn't, take the problem to your armorer.

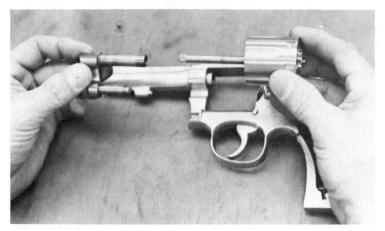

Once the yoke is clear of both cylinder and frame, they can be removed without scratching the surface.

Even as simple a job as tightening the extractor rod must be done right, or you can foul up your gun quickly.

On Smith & Wesson revolvers, the front sideplate screw is the yoke screw. It is fitted to the individual gun. Remove it and keep it separate from other screws. Open the cylinder and hold it in place, while drawing the yoke forward and out of the frame. Now, put two or more dummy cartridges in the charge holes of the cylinder to protect the extractor pins, and hold the extractor rod in a vise, diagonally. Never put the knurled end in a vise. Then turn the cylinder *counterclockwise* to tighten the extractor rod.

Switching screws, using the vise improperly, failing to use a dummy round, all are opportunities for the untrained "gunsmith" to cause his gun to fail when he needs it most.

A policeman's gun is too important a tool to leave it to anything less than the best care it can get. It should be used on the target range fre-

Removing the cylinder for cleaning is sometimes necessary, and proper procedures should be followed. Note dummy round in cylinder to support extractor star. Cylinder pin is tightened by clamping it in a vise as shown. Never clamp down on the knurled end, pictured on right.

quently. When you shoot a lot, it's a good idea to use light, mid-range loads, to avoid the punishment of full power loads. It's much easier on you. And the gun should be kept clean.

If you're curious about what's under the sideplate, look at the cutaway poster on the classroom wall and leave any repair work to a factory-trained armorer.

3

Gun Skill Can Mean Survival

The way a policeman is trained to use his gun today, as compared with years ago, is as different as night and day—but too few cops know it. A police instructor friend of mine did his own informal survey and he said, "You'd be surprised how many training programs are run just as they were 20 years ago."

He offered his own theories why, but the important point is that new techniques and procedures are not filtering down to many of today's law enforcement officers.

From what my friend found, most policemen start with the basic National Match Course of bullseye shooting. This teaches them the fundamentals of position, sight picture, and trigger control. Frankly, you should never see a bullseye target—unless you've really never seen a gun before or your instructor uses it for a remedial exercise.

Then most policemen progress to the Practical Pistol Course, which introduces them to new positions, hip and point-shoulder shooting, strong hand–weak hand and barricade shooting. But even the PPC does little to prepare you for what you'll find in real-life shooting situations.

Too often, training ends there.

3.1 It's More than Marksmanship

It takes more sophisticated equipment to put a recruit through the next step of training. It involves that split-second decision of whether to shoot or not to shoot, recognizing a threat, coping with stress and firing under adverse conditions.

How many targets do you think you'll face straight ahead at eye level, bathed in light and in the open? That's how you find them on the range, but not on the street.

Charles L. Smith, former FBI firearms instructor and retired Director of the Smith & Wesson Academy, says the purpose of firearms training is to save lives. The officer who is well trained in the use — or non-use — of his sidearm and is confident of his skill is less likely to be involved in a lethal situation.

3.2 Programs Are Changing

Training must prepare the officer for situations he'll face in real life.

Officer Survival is a new step in firearms training. It puts you through realistic, though simulated, scenarios. It reinforces the basics learned in the usual range sessions and adds new considerations. It gets into instinctive shooting.

Shoot and no-shoot targets present realistic challenges. Shown is a simple set-up on a standard range. Note use of cover by the officer on right.

What is the hardly visible target that pops out from behind the post? Is it a man with a gun, or a man with a camera in his hand? Don't forget your partner, and where is he? Lt. Michael Beckley of the Nassau County (New York) Police Department (partially shown, left foreground) set up this practical tactical situation and runs a two-man team of officers through it—together. They must use cover, work in unison, identify the threat level of the targets presented, and respond properly. Note that with the two men shooting, Beckley uses an assistant instructor, who watches in the right foreground. *Ted Morehead Photo.*

"Adam 12" taught us that most hollow core doors won't stop a bullet, but how many TV cops have you seen inching their way along a wall? A bullet that hits a hard wall doesn't bounce like a billiard ball. It skims along the wall about three inches away—right about where your heart is.

If you must return a felon's fire, you surely don't assume the proper stance, take aim and squeeze the trigger. You dive for whatever cover is available. Return fire can come only from a live cop.

Handgun retention is another new training consideration developed by James Lindell of the Kansas City (Missouri) Regional Police Training Academy, and adopted by the Kansas City Police in 1976. It teaches you how to use leverage, balance, and body mechanics to avoid being disarmed.

3.3 IALEFI Formed

These are all changes in the curricula of police training academies over just the past few years. They are all things you should know. The need to update training procedures led Charlie Smith to help organize the International Association of Law Enforcement Firearms Instructors, which provides information designed to help every firearms instructor improve his program. If your instructor is not a member, suggest that he write IALEFI, (P.O. Box 598, Brookline Village, MA 02147-0598) for an application.

4

Shooting Skill Means
More than Bullseyes

"Ready on the right. Ready on the left. Ready on the firing line." But on the street, who's calling range commands?

"With six rounds, load and holster." In one infamous shooting incident, a dead officer was found with five rounds in his open cylinder and one in his hand. No speedloaders.

"Police your brass before moving to the next position." Another dead officer was found to have six empty cartridge cases in his pocket.

That's how they were trained to do it, *on the range.*

4.1 Old Range Habits Were Deadly

The first officer had fumbled to get that sixth round into his gun, rather than keeping his eyes on his adversary. It never occurred to him that he could close the partially refilled cylinder and put three, four, or five rounds into the attacker before that one fatal shot got him. Since then, the department involved has adopted speedloaders.

The second officer had taken the time to dump the empties into his palm and pocket them before he ever reached for live ammunition for reloading.

When you are trained to handle a gun in a certain way, that's the way you react when required to do it instinctively. Range habits are hard to break. They may make life easier on the range, but they can be deadly on the street. And there are dead cops to prove it.

4.2 The Newhall Incident

In the infamous "Newhall Incident" (1970), four young California Highway Patrolmen died in a savage gunbattle that shocked the nation, one that was more bloody than the 1881 shoot-out at the OK Corral. Newhall was a sobering slap in the face for police firearms training, which simply had not kept pace with the escalating violence of the modern criminal element. In many ways, says police firearms writer Massad Ayoob, "The officer survival movement of today may largely be traced to the dearly

When you roll into a critical situation, the perfect positions learned on the range are not really forgotten. Note that Lt. Joel Kent of the Windsor (Connecticut) Police Department uses a good kneeling position while he takes advantage of the cover the cruiser provides.

expensive lessons learned that night in Newhall. Thus, the four martyred patrolmen did not die in vain."

Ayoob says the lessons learned from the experience of those four officers led to a seven-step guideline for handling felony stops, developed by the California Highway Patrol and given in the acronym NEWHALL.

N: Never approach until all perpetrators are in plain sight.

E: Evaluate the nature of the offense and the danger.

W: Wait for backup.

H: Have a plan for dealing with violent response.

A: Always maintain the advantage, and avoid one-on-one confrontations.

L: Look for the unusual.

L: Leave the scene if necessary, taking a safer and more dominant tactical position.

Police firearms training *is* changing. But changes take time. New ideas need to filter down before they are adopted by everyone. Firearms training for most policemen has yet to progress beyond the PPC.

4.3 Basic Training Is Important

I don't mean to play down the importance of basic training. Bullseye-style shooting still is useful for learning stance, breath control, sight picture, and trigger squeeze. You must make a habit of the *basics* of good shooting before you can consciously forget them, yet apply them instinctively whenever you shoot. PPC provides the more advanced techniques of double-action shooting, speed loading, the use of cover, and hip and point-shoulder shooting.

But PPC is not the end of firearms training, not by a long shot.

Part of using your firearm properly is knowing *if* it should be used. Recognizing a threat is the prime factor in your shooting decision, especially when you're before the Firearms Review Board. Recognizing different threat levels of multiple targets could be critical. Coping with stress improves your chances. In a close quarter situation, it just might be better to take an assailant's gun away from him, rather than try to draw your own gun.

How will an officer react if he is trained to respond only with his sidearm? Firearms training today means much more than just shooting skills.

This may be academic to graduates of modern police training programs, who don't have much choice in how they are trained. Admittedly, scoring your handgun proficiency is still most easily done by counting the "K" hits on the silhouette, or the number of shots you placed in the "X" ring. Range safety demands certain regimentation, and today's firearms instructors are learning to accommodate safety while instilling "street habits" into their students. A wise professor once said, "Teachers don't teach. They help the student learn." So the benefits of training depend on *you*, and your overall attitude.

4.4 Habits Depend on You

Qualification on the range may require that you score 210 points out of a possible 300 over the PCC; but the *real* measure of your success is how you handle yourself doing it. Whether it's required or not, you can help break certain range habits by attacking the course just as you would on the street. Dump the brass on the ground with your left hand as your right hand reaches for reloads. Then drop your speedloader. Keep your eyes on the target while reloading. Practice reloading blindfolded. Chose cover over concealment, if you can, and use it like you mean it. I'd rather have my wife wash my trousers after target practice than test her sewing skills in repairing a bullet hole after a gun battle.

Required qualification may be a chore, if you view it that way. But you can make it an asset. You can use it to develop habits that could well save your life one day. It all depends on your attitude and what you consider to be the purpose of your firearms training and qualification.

You can bet that my attitude is a craving to learn and practice all those little things that add up to *survival*—the real name of the game.

5

Police Are More than Pistols

The policeman is always pictured with his pistol; but there's an arsenal of alternate weapons he must know how to use.

Local television recently showed teams of policemen scouring the neighborhood for a guy who blew away his ex-girl friend after an argument and then escaped on foot. Most of the cops were carrying shotguns.

We had another recent case in a nearby jurisdiction where a patrol officer stopped a car matching the description of one used in an armed robbery. Even the description of the occupants matched. Police surrounded the pair while an officer checked them out. One of the policemen was holding a shotgun. The shotgun discharged accidentally, as the Firearms Review Board later determined, and the suspect became a "victim" because his only offense was matching the description. He was not the robber.

The furor that followed asked such questions as "How familiar was the officer with the shotgun?" and "How well trained was he in handling the shotgun he was issued?"

The answers too often are embarrassing.

5.1 The Cop IS a Hunter

Unless you are a hunter accustomed to carrying a loaded shotgun around all day, the times that you have the gun in hand are usually under

Sgt. Raymond Whitney of the Springfield (Massachusetts) Police Department demonstrates use of alternate cover with the shotgun. He can also use the vehicle's hood, which is even better.

stress. "Qualification" with the shotgun may consist of shucking a few shells through the pump gun at a cardboard target and a demonstration of how to load and unload the gun.

But you probably are not proficient in handling the shotgun off the firing range.

The hunter develops habits that make his gun safe until a bird flushes. The policeman searching with a shotgun in hand is doing the same thing as the hunter; so the same rules apply.

Point your shotgun in a safe direction. It's quite disconcerting to see that big 12-gauge hole aiming your way. When the situation is at ease, there's no gun safer than one with the action open. It takes only a second to close it when you need it.

5.2 Handling the Shotgun

While there are many different styles of shotguns, the police officer is most likely equipped with a 12-gauge, pump action shotgun with an 18- or 20-inch barrel. It may have a regular wood stock, folding stock, or just a pistol grip. It may have a bead front sight on a shot barrel, or rifle sights on a slug barrel.

When the gun is loaded and the action closed with a shell in the chamber, the safety must be "on." You're still careful where you point it because a safety is only a mechanical device, subject to wear and malfunction, and not a substitute for good gun manners.

It's a personal preference of mine to carry the shotgun with the magazine loaded and the action uncocked and closed on an empty chamber. The gun won't go off accidentally. When the situation tenses, racking the action to load the chamber takes but a split second. And that sound has probably stopped more thoughts of aggression than any other. The click of the safety being pushed "off" is virtually soundless.

5.2.1 Carrying the Shotgun

When carrying the shotgun while hunting for a fugitive, the officer should employ the same safety precautions as does the sportsman.

1. Never point it at anything you don't want to shoot.
2. Keep the safety on until ready to fire.

Should the chamber be loaded? Obviously, for fastest response, the shotgun needs to be carried with a shell in the chamber and the safety "on." But a safety is a mechanical device subject to wear and failure. It should never be the sole basis for safety.

Do what a hunter does:

1. Crook the gun over your strong arm, butt under your armpit, muzzle down and in front where you can see it.
2. Crook the gun over your weak side arm, with your hand covering the trigger guard, muzzle up and to the side where you can't see it.

When the situation tenses, the "ready position" is called for and puts you in position for a quick reaction.

5.2.2 Mounting the Gun

The officer carrying a shotgun in pursuit of a fugitive can use the same basic carries as does the hunter if the situation is at ease. But when a threat is potentially likely, the "ready position" is best. Then the shotgun is held in both hands, pointing ahead (as in bayonet drill). Keep the front bead in your line of sight. When it comes time to fire, bring the stock up to your cheek, pivot on the front bead, pull the stock back into the hollow of your shoulder, point and fire.

Only through much practice will you develop the ability to bring the shotgun into firing position, virtually on target. The secret is to focus your attention on the target and pivot on that front bead. Remember, with the

The casual hunter's carry with the shotgun allows you to see where the muzzle is pointing. Action open.

gun in the proper position, you should not see the top of the barrel with the shooting eye. If you do, the gun is too low on your shoulder.

5.2.3 Pointing the Shotgun

The shooter looks at the target along the top of the shotgun barrel. Thus, you are not aiming the gun but pointing it much as you would point

This is also an "approved" carry, with the muzzle pointed up while the hand covers the trigger guard. Action open.

your finger. Keeping both eyes open provides you with the widest peripheral vision to detect new threats off to either side. Because the shotgun is pointed rather than aimed, it is an effective weapon for dim light situations.

5.3 Shooting the Shotgun

Shooting the shotgun should be a natural thing for you to do. If you can point your finger, you certainly can point a shotgun. It's when you pull the trigger that your shooting skills come into play.

When you're in an attitude of impending threat, carry the shotgun in this "ready" position. Front bead sight is at eye level. Action is closed, gun loaded.

Bring the butt of the gun up to your cheek and back into your shoulder to get off a quick, well-pointed shot.

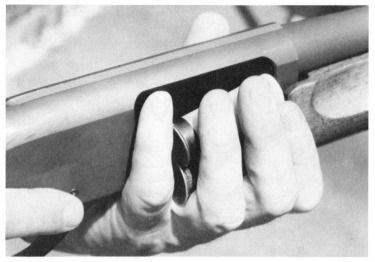

You can speedload a shotgun by holding two shells, bases to the rear; drop one into the ejection port and close the action.

The second shell is now right in position to feed it into the magazine, below.

5.3.1 Trigger Slap

The desirable trigger action with a shotgun is better described as a "slap." Trigger control is much the same as you will learn in practical pistol shooting.

5.3.2 Lead and Swing

When shooting at a moving target, lead the target to compensate for the time it takes for the shot to travel from the gun to the target. It's like a paint brush. The brush actually points ahead of where the ends of the bristles touch the surface.

Rather than hold a calculated lead on a moving target, you can compensate for the variables automatically by pacing the speed of the gun swing slightly faster than the apparent speed of the target. Slap the trigger as the gun passes through the target, continuing a smooth swing. It's called "swing through."

5.3.3 Follow Through

A smooth continuous motion is as important to good shooting as it is to good golf, tennis, or baseball. It becomes even more critical in applying "swing through" on a moving target. Proper follow through provides the lead needed to put the shot on target.

5.3.4 Hip Shooting

It used to be taught that from the "port arms" position it's faster to deliver a close range shot from the hip. Using the same grip on the gun, just straighten your left arm. The right elbow locks the stock of the gun into your side and the right forearm is parallel to the ground. Thus, the gun is level and can be pointed with good accuracy at close ranges. This isn't something you'd normally do with a shotgun, but it could be used for a reactive shot if you are jumped.

If you're in a vulnerable position, you should use the "ready position." Then it's fastest to simply bring the stock to your cheek, pivot on the front bead, and fire.

5.3.5 Skip Firing

The fact that a projectile does not ricochet like a billiard ball, but travels a few inches away from a hard surface, taught us never to inch along an alley wall. This same characteristic can be used against a subject hiding behind an automobile—or inching along an alley wall.

Skip firing refers to ricocheting a shot charge off the street in front of the intended target. It can be used against the felon shooting at you from behind an automobile with his feet and ankles exposed if he's standing between the tires. Skip firing does not necessarily reduce the possibility of inflicting fatal wounds. The shotgun should never be used to "punish" an offender. It is used *only* when deadly force is justified.

5.3.6 Unloading the Shotgun

The shotgun must be unloaded and action left open before cleaning or passing it to another person on the range. This is done by opening the action just enough to clear the extracted round from the chamber, pushing the lifter up, then tripping the shell stop(s) with the fingernail to pop shells from the magazine tube one by one. Different shotguns may require different procedures (some have two shell stops), but the same principles apply.

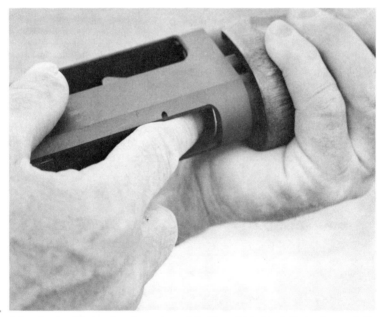

After clearing the chambered round, reach inside and trip the shell stop to pop shells from the magazine, one-by-one.

5.4 Clearing a Jam

With the reliability of modern pump guns, you should never experience a jam. Just work the action purposefully and smoothly. Don't baby it. Even the horror of a shell slipped back under the lifter can be cleared by a bit of judicial abuse. One police firearms instructor taught me to hold the fore-end and slam the butt against a brick wall. Sideways, of course. But some newer-design shotguns avoid this potential problem.

At the SHOT Show in Atlanta in 1982, Smith & Wesson's eastern regional manager for law enforcement, Tom Madden, demonstrated the then-new Model 3000 Police shotgun. He loaded a dummy shell into the chamber and closed the action. Then he stuffed another dummy into the magazine tube and tripped the shell so that the second shell slipped back into the action between the lifter and the bolt.

"You've had it now," I said.

He just smiled as he "fired" the shell in the chamber, racked the action, and "fired" the second shell that supposedly had jammed the action. The key is to rack the action with purpose.

Work the action of a shotgun with purpose and you'll avoid problems. Never "baby" a shotgun action. That leads to "short stroking" the action, which can miss the shell on the lifter and not chamber it.

The point of this example is that the policeman wears his *sidearm* at all times. He loads and unloads it every day. He can "dry fire" it in front of the bedroom mirror if he's conscientious. He fires a full qualification course regularly. He is familiar with his handgun. But the *shotgun* stays locked in the rack in the cruiser. Even if he must remove it and unload it after his patrol, he still doesn't get much chance to shoot it on the range. He gets little chance to become really familiar with it.

Yet the shotgun is a patrol weapon, not one of those special weapons reserved for specially trained units. And it takes practice to handle it, professionally.

6

Handling the Handgun

If you were in the armed forces, you've had a basic course in shooting. Even if you weren't, there's no point in preaching a "sermon" about the major parts of the pistol (nomenclature, they call it) or leading you step-by-step through a bunch of boring details. I'll leave that to your firearms instructor.

For the most part, remember that the proper shooting positions, stances, and such are what feels *natural* to you. You shouldn't conform to rigid rules, such as the competitive shooter does. Your firearms instructor can show you in one minute what would take many pages to do here.

We'll discuss all the things you should know about shooting to help you understand them better. But the key person is your firearms instructor. Ask him questions. He can spot your mistakes and help you to correct them. Take every advantage of your time with him. Remember, the only dumb question is the one you don't ask.

The firearm is so basic to officer survival that its use must be natural and instinctive, requiring no conscious thought.

If you are confident in your skill with your gun, you can take that extra split second to focus attention on the critical decision of whether to shoot or not. Bad shooting situations happen to those who are so unsure of themselves that they shoot too quickly. Good shooting situations result when you immediately – and instinctively – recognize the danger signs, and react the way you should.

6.1 Good Gun Habits

Safety is not a separate subject, especially where firearms are concerned. It's part of "proper gun handling." If something is unsafe, it is improper. It's impolite to point, my mother always told me. It's especially impolite when you have a gun in your hand – unless you are pointing for a purpose. So:

1. Treat every gun as if it were loaded. Yours is. It's the other "unloaded" gun that you always hear about being involved in accidents.

2. Open the action. Swing out the cylinder. Lock the auto slide back. Open the rifle or shotgun bolt. Always pass a firearm to another person with the action open. The only time you really know a gun can't fire is when the action is open.

3. Point the gun only at something you intend to shoot. The muzzle of the gun should always be directed where, if it were to discharge accidentally, it would cause no serious damage or injury.

4. Keep your finger out of the trigger guard unless you intend to pull the trigger. Develop the habit of handling your revolver with the trigger finger extended alongside the trigger guard. If your finger is on the trigger, a stumble with gun in hand could cause an accidental discharge. You'll need this habit when you get into combat shooting.

5. Horseplay belongs to horses, not policemen. Your revolver is not a conversation piece or a string of worry beads.

6. Take care of your sidearm and it will take care of you when you need it most.

6.2 Guns at Home

There is no single best answer to keeping guns in the home, especially for the police officer. If there are kids around, hunting guns should be unloaded and stored in a locked rack or cabinet. Ammunition should be locked away separately in a drawer or cabinet. Some people maintain that *all* guns and ammunition should be locked away separately, out of sight. But that's like having no gun at all should an emergency arise.

If you leave a revolver at home alone, a padlock or handcuffs locked through the topstrap of an open cylinder prevents it from being closed. If children are old enough to understand, they should be taught to respect the power potential of your firearm. Satisfy their curiosity at a safe range in a way that will engender respect. I raised three boys in a house full of guns.

With cylinder open, place one cuff around topstrap, so that cylinder won't close. The other cuff, placed behind the trigger, prevents it from reaching its rearmost position, where it would release the sear. There's no way this gun can fire. It would, however, take you a while to free it from its "safety" if you should need it in a hurry. If you must leave your gun where it could be accessible to others, this procedure is a mighty safe one.

Each had been to the range and seen what a bullet will do to an oil can filled with water.

6.3 Guns on the Range

Much of what has been written in the form of range safety rules is now outdated. You may have to reload without command. You may have to holster a loaded revolver. But proper gun handling always applies. You should be familiar with range commands and *instantly* obey the command to "cease firing." At the National Matches at Camp Perry, Ohio, this command rang out one year most unexpectedly. A target pit crew had started marching right across the range. The range officer is in command of his range, no matter who is on the firing line. Follow whatever rules he has posted or commands he issues on the range.

Though rare, there are such things as hangfires, misfires, and squib—or super-light—loads. If a shot doesn't *sound* right, stop shooting, keep the muzzle pointed downrange, and signal for a range officer.

6.4 Nomenclature

Every police officer should know the names of the major parts of a firearm and ammunition components. Check the posters on the range wall and be able to identify the following:

Barrel	Firing pin
Frame or Receiver	Stock and Fore-end
Action	Magazine
Grip	Magazine release
Butt	Trigger
Muzzle	Trigger guard
Cylinder	Safety
Slide	Ejector
Thumb latch	Hammer
Slide lock	Cartridge Case
Extractor	Bullet
Sights	Primer
Chamber	Powder

6.5 Handgun Techniques

While the techniques of the target shooter are designed for precision rather than practical shooting, they provide you with a better understanding of fundamentals. Basic errors are easier to spot and correct before they become bad habits. Once the fundamentals of accurate shooting become habit, you won't have to think about them when you graduate to practical shooting.

When shooting single-action, for example, you can easily see the necessity for proper grip, sight alignment, breath control, trigger control, sight picture, and follow through. And it is possible that you might be called upon one day to deliver an accurately placed shot at 50 yards.

6.5.1 Grip

In target shooting, new shooters tend to grip the gun too tightly, causing a tremor that makes proper sight alignment difficult. The target shooter places the gun in his shooting hand with his weak hand—fully back into the web of the hand with the weight of the revolver resting on the middle finger. This positions the revolver in a straight line with the forearm so that, with the wrist locked, the gun becomes an extension of the forearm. This becomes critical when you get into combat shooting. The gun *feels* right with the proper grip.

The grip is essentially the same for either precision or practical shooting, except that in precision shooting, your thumb is extended forward and upward along the frame of the gun. The combat grip locks the thumb *down* onto the finger below. Use of a grip adapter or combat style stocks is recommended.

6.5.2 Two-Hand Grip

The shooting hand takes the same grip as in the one-hand grip. The weak hand is brought up to the gun, fingers wrapping around the fingers of the shooting hand. The support hand thumb, hooked over the shooting hand thumb, helps lock the grip. Strength of grip is provided by the shooting hand. An automatic pistol with a hooked trigger guard enables your weak hand finger to wrap over it and help hold the muzzle down in recoil. The weak hand provides support.

The two-hand grip with a revolver uses the support-hand thumb locked over the shooting-hand thumb, to help control the gun during recoil.

With an auto, having a trigger guard hook, the support-hand index finger controls recoil. Don't wrap your weak thumb over your wrist; if you do, the recoiling slide will put railroad tracks on your thumb, which will be painful and cause flinching.

6.5.3 Stance

The target shooter's unsupported standing position has no application in police work so, although an instructor may use it for remedial training, it usually is not taught.

Until recently, officers were taught the isosceles triangle stance facing the target squarely. This is an erect position with both arms locked straight, forming an isosceles triangle with the line of the shoulders.

The preferable stance today—the Weaver stance—has the shooter quartering the target toward the strong side. The weak arm is bent. The strong arm is slightly bent and pushes across your chest, while the weak hand pulls slightly. This push-pull action provides a more stable isometric platform for the gun and can be adapted to most positions when you get into combat or practical shooting.

6.5.4 Sight Alignment

In both precision and practical shooting, sight alignment is of utmost importance. This is the alignment of the front and rear sights, disregarding the target. Your sights are perhaps six inches apart. A 1/10th-inch error in

The traditional isosceles-triangle point-shoulder position permits a wide traverse. Both arms are extended, gun at eye level.

sight alignment increases that same amount for every six inches the bullet travels. Thus, at 50 yards, that "tiny" misalignment adds up to an error of 30 inches at the target — enough to miss a man. If sight alignment is exact, you can waver through a considerable distance and still deliver your shot on target.

6.5.5 Sight Picture

Adding the target completes the sight picture. In bullseye-style shooting, the target shooter usually sights in his revolver for a 25-yard, 6 o'clock

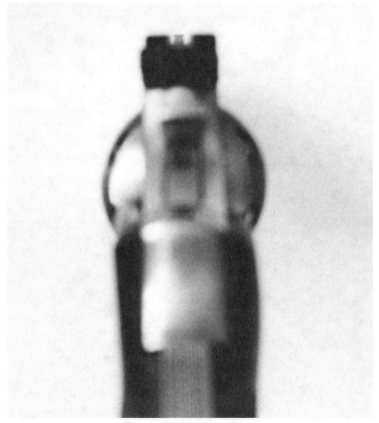

You should focus your eye on the front sight so that you can center it precisely in the rear notch, as shown here.

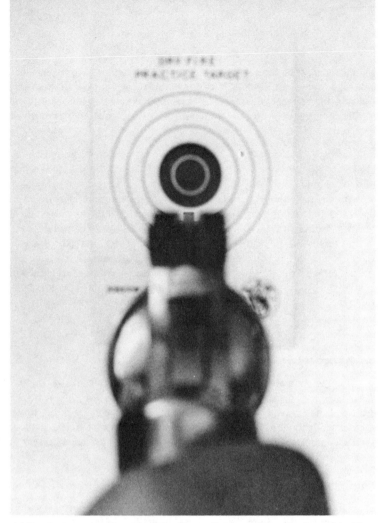

Adding the target completes the sight picture; focus remains on the front sight. Even though the target may seem blurred, you still know where it is, and your bullet should hit the bullseye.

hold (the bullseye sits on the front sight like a pumpkin on a fence post), so that he can hold point-of-aim at 50 yards. This provides a more precise sight picture on the round bullseye at 25 yards and avoids the need to change the sights for 50 yards.

The target shooter will focus his eye on the front sight rather than the target. That demonstrates how critical is sight alignment, the importance of which increases as the range increases. From the 3½ yard line, the front sight is the most important element. If it's on target, that's where your shot will be. From about 10 yards back, however, focus your eye on the front sight for the best sight alignment. The target may be fuzzy but you can see it. Once you make proper sight alignment a habit, you can afford quick glances at the target.

6.5.6 Breath Control

Breathing properly is critical to precision shooting and certainly influences practical shooting accuracy. Once you learn to apply breath control, you won't have to think about it any more; it will come naturally.

In target shooting, the firer takes a normal breath, lets part of it out, then holds it as he acquires the proper sight picture and slowly squeezes the trigger until the shot lets-off right on target. Developing this habit will enable you to simply stop breathing as you fire, without any conscious thought during the process. Controlled breathing, while firing, enhances basic steadiness.

6.5.7 Trigger Control

Trigger control for the police officer is best described as a smooth "stroke" of the trigger with steadily increasing pressure directly toward the rear, with no influence to either side. Don't let your trigger finger touch the frame of your gun. Your trigger finger should contact the trigger at about the first knuckle. Speed of the trigger pull increases as range decreases.

6.5.8 Follow Through

Follow through is stressed in shooting – as it is in most sports – simply to avoid the disruption of a sudden movement before the action of firing is completed.

Proper follow through enables you to "call the shot." This means that your brain retains a mental image of the sights at the instant of firing. You just know where your shot hit, even before you check the target. Without follow through, you don't know where your shot went; more than likely you jerked the trigger, or "heeled" the gun, deflecting the shot off to one side or the other.

Your firearms instructor may use a variety of exercises to detect and resolve certain shooting problems, such as dry-firing, ball and dummy, triangulation, or wax bullet loads.

6.6 Shooting Positions

Rather than the target shooter's standing offhand position, you'll probably learn the Weaver stance. Quarter the target toward the strong side, feet comfortably apart — the standard "interview" position when you are talking with a subject. The revolver is drawn in one smooth motion and thrust forward, bringing it up to eye level. The weak arm comes up at the same time but remains bent, providing the two-hand grip. Other shooting positions will be discussed in the practical shooting section.

6.7 Your Gun Needs Care

Your handgun is not like a sporting arm that spends most of its time in a cabinet or case. It rides by your side every day, through all kinds of weather. With proper care, your gun will last a lifetime. "Proper care" means knowing when, why, and how to clean your gun. Improper cleaning can cause wear or damage when you need it least.

Clean your gun after every range session and exposure to bad weather or high humidity.

The bore must be cleaned from the muzzle, so use only a proper size cleaning rod to avoid damaging the bore up front. Clean all cylinder holes from the breech end, with proper size patches.

Use a bronze or brass brush to remove leading every time you clean. Residues may be cleaned from the barrel throat, yoke, underside of the topstrap, and cylinder with a lint-free cloth or patch and powder solvent.

Remember that oil is like castor oil — a little is good, but a lot can be painful.

7

How Well Will You Survive?

Old habits die hard. While police firearms training is changing drastically nowadays, it takes time for new programs to filter down. Meanwhile, you're still faced with the need to survive the unexpected threat.

So, you've fired the PPC; so often that you have no problem qualifying Expert. It's become habit. That's fine, as far as it goes. But will you do the same thing when you get into a firefight on the street?

The statistically average firefight happens with the adversary less than 20 feet away; a total of 2.3 shots are fired in 2.7 seconds. And it's likely dusk, so your sights aren't much help.

The PPC doesn't prepare you for *that*.

7.1 Street Situations

Shootings occur under stress. There are distractions. The adrenalin is pumping. You're out of breath. What does that do to your qualification scores?

My department's firearms instructor thinks something is wrong if he scores only 295 x 300 over the PPC. He was invited to test fire the new stress course conducted by the nearby Hartford (Connecticut) Police Academy.

He scored 220. Result: we have developed a new stress course for our department.

The point is that unless you have access to a progressive training academy, your firearms skills probably are not in tune with the close, fast, and dirty situations you're likely to face in real life.

7.1.1 IPSC

International Practical Shooting Confederation (IPSC) competitions are designed to induce stress by presenting multiple targets, making *time* part of your score rather than just a limit, putting you into awkward positions, and requiring movement from one shooting position to another.

Such modest exertion had me puffing, and my heart was pounding as if I'd scaled Mt. Everest. So there must have been more than just physical activity. There must have been *mental* stress.

I started shooting IPSC matches because they seem to relate better to the challenges that an officer might face on the street. Its courses of fire are ever-changing. If you can score reasonably well under such stressful situations, you're probably a survivor.

But what about the "meantime?" How well prepared are you to survive the unexpected?

7.1.2 Self Evaluation

The U.S. Region of IPSC publishes the *Practical Shooting Course Book*, which includes an interesting exercise called "Short Range Interpersonal Crisis Management Evaluation." All you need is a safe place to shoot, a friend with a stopwatch, and two targets set 18 inches apart. You shoot four shots in each of four stages, two shots at each target. But for each stage, you start facing a different direction—left, right and, finally, with your back to the target. Total score, minus 10 penalty points for each miss, divided by the total time, multiplied by the relative stopping power factor of the load you're using gives you a *survival index*.

If you want the book, write to A-Zone Publishing, Box 626, Sioux City, IA 51102.

Running through the exercise informally will give you the basic IPSC approach to this type of marksmanship, described in detail in the book.

7.1.3 Practical Shooting Is Different

The difference between disciplines is that competition and qualification are *precision* shooting, while gunfights are *practical* shooting. To achieve a high score on qualification, you apply precision shooting techniques. But try shooting a precision course at twilight — without lights.

When I was a kid, our target practice was done with a scope-sighted .22 rifle at the town dump. We kept the rat population down. My ability to quickly shoulder a deer rifle, and have the scope virtually on target, I attribute to those days down in the dump.

One day we found a carton of medicine vials. But we didn't want to walk out into the trash to set them up. So we shot them on the wing. Holding the rifle waist high, we tossed the vials straight out, brought the rifle up, and fired. It didn't take long before we were hip shooting the rifle, keeping our eyes on the target, and breaking the vials every time.

The late Herb Parsons, the famous Winchester exhibition shooter, called it "instinctive" shooting. I prefer to call it inherent ability. Anyone can point his finger at something. Anyone can learn practical shooting — if he tries.

But remember we added a different factor for the policeman. You're facing a holed-up "suspect." Shots have been fired. You move to a better position and are about ready to fire. A backup officer arrives with lights flashing. People are hollering. Total confusion.

You face distraction.

If you have no opportunity to train under stress, it's well worth your while to set up your own stress situation.

7.2 Do-It-Yourself Training

At a range or sand pit, instead of evenly spaced targets, bunch two or three targets in groups and space the groups out along the target line. At one side you can have an old car. Set up a wall in front of one group of targets, a cardboard "mailbox" in front of another. A railroad tie can play a curb, and try shooting over that when you have to lie parallel to keep your body behind cover. Set up the shooting positions so that you have to run from one to another. Introduce obstacles such as a sawhorse to crawl under, a fence to climb over. Then time the whole thing from start to finish. No time out to reload, and you'd better reload behind cover. You can put in some "hostage" targets and hope you don't shoot one.

When you've gotten smug because you ran the course with wadcutters, run it again with full service loads. When you score all K5s because you're applying those precision shooting techniques, wait until the sun goes down. Then try again and again, each time striving to better your last score.

Don't forget the distractions. They're important. Have a couple of friends holler at each other at the top of their voices while you're trying to concentrate on shooting. Have someone blow a horn, pop a paper bag,

This IPSC match at the Agawam (Massachusetts) Pistol Club shows how multiple targets can be presented under adverse shooting conditions.

create diversion. But never allow anyone to "attack" the shooter. He must keep his gun pointed downrange at all times. In the heat of the moment, he could react to a threat from behind.

There you have a shopping list of ideas you may see in an IPSC match, or during a stress course. They're all elements that cops concerned with self-preservation can do on their own—to help save their lives.

Combat Shooting

Once you understand the basics of revolver shooting, it's necessary to develop those skills to meet the practical demands of challenges you face on the street. You must instinctively respond to a threat in a proper manner. So, you need to:

    1. Apply basic shooting skills to street situations.

    2. Develop practical shooting skills.

8.1 Practical Skills

This discussion will include new techniques developed by recognized experts in police firearms training and now being taught by the FBI. Remember, you should be exposed to normal and dim light conditions in a variety of circumstances. You should fire *only* double-action. The gun is gripped naturally but firmly with the thumb locked down onto the finger, and the trigger finger is thrust through the trigger guard, contacting the trigger at the first knuckle or nearly so. A locked wrist is part of a proper grip. The two-hand grip should be used in other than close combat and hip-crouch positions.

8.1.1 Trigger Control

Trigger control in double-action shooting should be a smooth pull directly to the rear until the revolver fires. When shooting multiple shots, never allow the trigger to rest in its forward position. As soon as you release it after your first shot, start back on the trigger again as you pick up your sights.

8.1.2 Sighting

The proper sight picture may be checked only with peripheral vision in some close quarter situations. But then there's a difference of opinion. Some instructors say that even when sights are used, your attention should be focused on the target. Some argue that sight alignment is so important

When you look "through" the sights at the target, the sights are blurred. This front sight is offset a bit to the left. You're better off focusing on the front sight, to keep alignment exact.

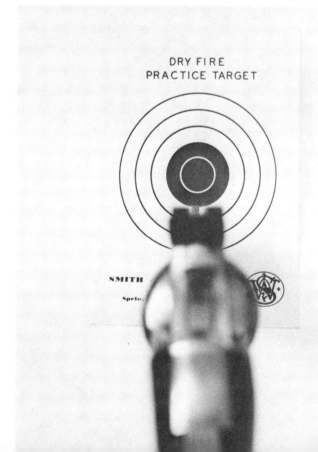

DRY FIRE
PRACTICE TARGET

SMITH

Sprin

that you should always focus on the front sight. At ranges of 25 yards or more, you have to focus your eye on the sights just before firing for your shot to be accurately placed. If you've ever read a newspaper while watching television, you know what I mean.

8.1.3 Weak Hand

It is unlikely that you will ever have to shoot with your weak hand. But there are situations where use of the weak hand may be preferred, such as weak-side barricade, to avoid exposing any more of your body than necessary. Weak-hand shooting is included to give you confidence in your ability to return fire under difficult circumstances.

In a special course I recently completed with the revolver, two stages of fire included six shots weak-hand Weaver stance. I was surprised how well I did. I had to squint my dominant right eye to sight with the left, but I got sharp sight alignment—and a few flyers.

Getting into a weak-hand Weaver stance involved simply transferring the gun to the weak hand, stepping back with the weak foot, and taking up a mirror image position. You'll be surprised how well you can do, too.

8.1.4 Draw

The draw is done in one smooth motion. Reach for the gun in the holster, and unsnap the retaining device with the thumb or index finger, depending upon holster design. Grasp the grip firmly with the thumb and three fingers so that the gun and forearm form a straight, steel-stiff line. Lift the gun out of the holster and straighten your wrist. (Those of us who wear a security holster can't do it as smoothly as those who wear a Jordan-style holster.) The trigger finger should be extended forward alongside the trigger guard. Punch the gun in a straight line up to eye level. Your weak hand is waiting at about midpoint and wraps around the gun hand. As the gun comes into the field of peripheral vision, the trigger finger is thrust through the trigger guard, and the trigger pull is completed as the gun is leveled at the target.

8.2 Weaver Stance

For two-hand shooting, the Weaver stance is preferred by many instructors because it allows quicker recovery from recoil, and more closely approximates a position you would naturally assume under street conditions.

Not everyone, however, is sold on the merits of the Weaver stance. One instructor I know argues that the isosceles triangle stance feels more natural.

S&W Academy instructor Hank Kudlinski demonstrates the draw-and-fire sequence now being taught almost universally. First, get a grip on your gun while it's in the holster.

Bring the gun up, and straighten your wrist.

Punch the gun forward in a straight line toward the target. Your weak hand meets it halfway. Trigger pull begins about here, gradually.

You're in a Weaver stance as the gun reaches eye level, you pick up the front sight, and you complete the trigger pull, firing the gun.

"It's the position usually taken automatically in a moment of stress without thinking about it, and aids in shot placement during point-shoulder or dim light situations," he says.

For me, the Weaver stance feels more natural — once I trained out of the old habit of taking the isosceles triangle position every time I shot a handgun. The Weaver is more like the position you learned as a youngster, shooting a rifle or shotgun. It's more like the position you assume at the barricade. Your body is in the "interview" position with your gun side shielded from the suspect. Assuming the Weaver stance simply is faster than assuming the isosceles stance.

If you are thoroughly trained in one action, you do it naturally. You will revert to it until your new training overtakes the old habit and becomes the natural thing to do.

Sgt. Jack Weaver of the Los Angeles County Sheriff's Department developed the stance that bears his name some 20 years ago. He competed in the old Southwest Combat League and he won matches using his stance. My instructor friend argues that what wins matches on the range doesn't necessarily win gunfights on the street. He's right.

The one absolute fact presented here is that there is no absolute fact, no one-best-way for everyone when it comes to shooting. Your shooting position should feel natural to you and, if you score all K-zone hits with it, then it's right for you.

When you quarter the target in the Weaver stance, your shooting arm is extended — elbow slightly bent — across your chest, like a rifle. Your non-shooting hand is brought up to the gun and wraps around your shooting hand; one thumb locks down on your shooting hand thumb. Your non-shooting arm is bent to about a 90-degree angle, with the elbow pointing straight down. (When you arm wrestle, your arm is most stable when it is vertical. Right?)

You might be more accustomed to the old isosceles triangle stance, and if it works, fine. But, if you're open to new ideas, you may find the Weaver stance to be more comfortable and provide better control.

8.3 Shooting Positions

8.3.1 Close Combat

The Bill Jordan–developed *Close Combat* technique responds to a threat where you are standing at interview distance and you have neither room nor time to extend the revolver toward the subject. It begins from the normal interview position with your gun side quartered away from the subject.

The Weaver stance is more stable for rapid fire. Pushing with the gun hand and pulling with the support hand aids stability. But traverse toward the weak side is more limited. Since Hank Kudlinski showed a right-handed Weaver stance, left-hander Jerry Lane demonstrates his strong-side stance. Weak-hand shooting for a right-hander looks just like this. Front and side views shown.

When the subject, at arm's length distance, draws on you, his action has already started. Your reaction must be faster. But reaction is always slower than action. You must expedite that first shot, or it will be fired after the subject's first shot. You wouldn't want that to happen. So, simply rotate the revolver up and out of the holster into a level position close by your side. The weak hand may toss a notebook or whatever it is holding toward the subject's face to distract him. This causes an involuntary closing of the eyes. Trigger pull is completed as the gun is leveled.

8.3.2 Hip Level Crouch

The hip level crouch position is outdated by the Weaver stance, which is just as fast and has the advantage of a two-hand grip.

The crouch position was taught to respond to a threat from a subject standing close but beyond grabbing distance. As the revolver is drawn, the weak side foot is shifted outward and the knees bent to give you good balance. A good grip on the gun is critical. The revolver is drawn up and out of the holster, then jabbed forward as if giving a punch to the solar plexus. Many find it helpful to lock the elbow into the side with the forearm level. As the revolver comes into your peripheral vision (your attention is on the target, remember) the gun is fired. Again, the weak hand may toss whatever it's holding to distract the subject.

The crouch position was taught to provide fast reaction on the street. You could extend the revolver anywhere from hip level to nearly eye level, depending upon the time available. But I've come to believe that it's faster to stay in my "interview" position, draw into a Weaver stance, and put the shot right where I want it.

8.3.3 Point Shoulder

The old point-shoulder position is similar to the crouch position, except a two-hand grip is used, the back is more erect, and the revolver is brought up to nearly eye level. Eye focus remains on the target with the officer looking over the sights. The revolver is "pointed" rather than "aimed." That's the old style. But, I repeat, the Weaver stance is faster and more accurate for my money. And that's what counts.

8.3.4 Barricade

Shooting with support may involve any shooting position and many different forms of cover. Remember that "cover" provides some protection from returned fire. "Concealment" only hides you from view. Use it if you

If an attack comes from arm's distance, you were too close to begin with. The draw must be quicker. Kudlinski shows that you don't move far before the gun is fired. Bring the gun up out of the holster, level it, and fire as your non-gun hand pushes the assailant or throws whatever it was holding toward his eyes.

have nothing better available. You'd be surprised how people react when trying to shoot at something they can't see.

When shooting around the corner of a building with your strong hand, for example, the weak foot is forward to turn most of your body behind cover. The back of the weak hand, in the two-hand grip, is pressed against

Firing from behind cover offers little exposure. But Bob Hunt, formerly of Massachusetts State Police, emphasizes that there's something different about this "barricade" position. Someone hiding behind the downspout might grab your gun if it extends beyond the cover.

the support. Don't let the gun itself touch the barricade. It will throw you off balance. Note that this is essentially a Weaver stance.

What if someone is waiting just around the corner of that building? You could be in for a big surprise as your gun is wrenched from your grasp. On the street, use the barricade for cover; but stay back a few feet from the "barricade." From the target's view, it looks the same, but your gun is not within grabbing distance.

When shooting from the weak side, your grip and stance should be the mirror image of strong side shooting. Using the weak eye, if possible, affords greater protection.

8.3.5 Kneeling

When shooting from behind a mailbox or fire hydrant, the kneeling position is steadier and keeps more of your body behind cover. It gives you three points of contact with the ground; and a tripod is steadier than a bipod.

The weak side foot is moved forward, and the strong side knee drops to the ground. A two-hand grip is used.

Note that Hunt is back from the blind spot. If there were a surprise waiting, he could touch off several rounds before being grabbed.

Lane shows the high kneeling position that traverses more easily and affords, if need be, a quick getaway.

There are two kneeling positions. The "high" position has only the knee and feet touching the ground; it's like standing from the waist up. This is less stable but lets you traverse, move more quickly. The steadier "low" position puts your butt on the heel of your strong side foot, with the weak side elbow resting *over* the weak side knee. You can't rest a ball on a ball. With the ball of the elbow over the knee, your arm bone can fit into the hollow on the inside of the knee. You're less flexible, but more stable for a long shot. Note the similarity to the Weaver stance.

A variety of kneeling positions are shown by this group on the firing line. Note that some are lower than others, thus making smaller targets.

8.3.6 Sitting

This position is confining, and no longer used by the FBI and many other law enforcement agencies, except in rifle shooting.

It is assumed by dropping the buttocks to the ground (use weak hand for support) and the feet extended or crossed in front. The knees are drawn up so that both arms may be supported by the knees. Always assume the position before drawing your revolver, which you bring up to shooting position along the *outside* of the leg.

8.3.7 Prone

This position is assumed by dropping to both knees. Extending the non-shooting hand forward for support as you draw, lean forward and lower your body to the ground in one smooth motion.

The body angle should be about 45 degrees toward the strong side. The shooting arm is straight, weak arm bent. The shooter rolls toward the strong side to rest his cheek against the biceps of the shooting arm. Cock the weak knee up, lifting the weak side of the chest off the ground. Note the similarity to the Weaver stance.

This position is much more comfortable than the old straight prone, and permits more accurate shooting. The revolver may even be canted to get under a low barricade, or to shoot around a tire.

The rollover prone position is not just easier on your neck, it also takes advantage of any cover. You don't see much of Kudlinski behind the box.

Yet you see he is in a good rollover prone position. While he takes advantage of cover, it isn't allowed to interfere.

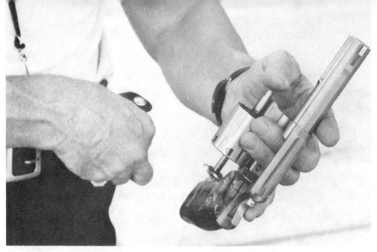

Reloading with speedloaders is a must if you shoot a revolver. Dump the empty brass straight to the ground while reaching for speedloader.

8.4 Reloading Procedures

A new aspect of police firearms training teaches you never to relax with an unloaded gun. As soon as you empty your gun, immediately reload and look at the target before you holster a *loaded* revolver. Thus, it is important to count your shots so that you know when to reload. If you forget, you may start the next string of fire – or face an adversary – with your empty gun.

Open the cylinder, using both hands. With your weak hand holding the cylinder and thumb on the ejector rod, dump the empty cases directly onto the ground as your strong hand reaches for a speedloader, or six fresh

With the muzzle down and holding the speedloader by its "barrel," start cartridges into cylinder, then slip fingers back to release twist knob on speedloader.

Note position of hands while reloading an auto. In the dark, the index finger helps guide the magazine into pistol grip.

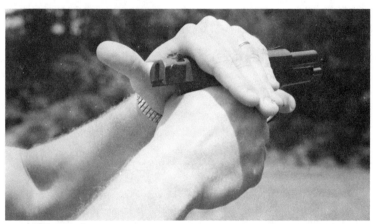

To clear a "stovepipe" jam, force the slide back with your weak hand. If this doesn't clear the gun, remove magazine.

rounds. Grasp your speedloader by its barrel, then slip your fingers back to the release knob, once the cartridges have started into the cylinder.

As soon as the cylinder is reloaded, let go of the speedloader as your weak hand's thumb closes the cylinder. Resume the proper grip with your strong hand. Your weak hand resumes the two-hand grip and you're ready to fire or reholster. But first, check your target, and those to either side, for a few seconds; you'd want to do that on the street, wouldn't you?

That's the point of everything you do on the range. You want to develop the *habits* that will keep you alive when the shooting's for real.

9

Improve Your Skills
and Have Fun, Too

There is a way you can have fun and become a more proficient policeman in the process. It means exerting yourself, but in a nice way. Calisthenics never excited me either; but an enjoyable hunt in rough country exercises muscles, too.

For your own survival, you need to be well-exercised in the use of your sidearm. But you could well be learning all the wrong habits.

Shooting at a bullseye target is a competition for NRA National Match Course (NMC) shooters. It is a training technique to implant the fundamentals firmly in your brain. The Practical Pistol Course (PPC) also is a teaching technique, and a competition. Both provide a competitive challenge to make them enjoyable. But some police instructors today are saying that neither really prepares you for the street.

The PPC is a convenient way to qualify a number of officers at the same time. But repeating a standard course of fire develops a deliberate response, a careful draw, and aimed first shot.

Writing in the *Wyoming Peace Officer*, Sgt. Mike Hanson of the Cody Police says, "The sad reality is that the officer comes away from these (training and qualification) sessions barely able to properly defend himself or someone else."

To avoid the "conditioned response" of repetitive courses, changes in shooting approaches must be made. You may face more than one adversary, in different directions, at different angles. If a shot has been fired at you, your "conditioned response" needs to get you behind cover. These and others are habits to be learned through dedication and application.

9.1 Practical Competition

The International Practical Shooting Confederation (IPSC) was founded by firearms trainers wanting a competitive program that more closely approximates the challenges one might face in real life. IPSC *is* attracting the attention of police officers.

"I've never fired a shot in competition before," said Sgt. Raymond Whitney of the Springfield (Massachusetts) Police. "But this IPSC style of shooting makes sense."

Whitney fired in a local IPSC match, once over the course with his duty gun in minor class and again with the .45 auto in major class. Courses of fire included a *Jungle Lane, Cooper Assault,* and *Columbia Fumble.* It doesn't matter if you know the exact program. It won't be run the same way the next time.

I shot the *Jungle Lane* first. My co-worker, Tom Campbell, one of the top IPSC shooters in the country, suggested it — probably to destroy my confidence, right off the bat. There were no more than 20 targets and 10 minutes to shoot them in, but Rangemaster Dwight Brouillard wouldn't say how long the course was. I think I saw about half the targets.

The *Cooper Assault* course required participants to fire two shots at each of two targets, leap a four-foot wall, fire two shots at each of two more targets, crawl through a 2½-foot high tunnel, fire two shots at a fifth target, then fire a shot on a steel plate to stop the clock.

The *Columbia Fumble* required participants to run and pick up a tin can with their gun hand and place it on a stake, then draw and fire two shots at each of three targets, and one on the steel plate to stop the clock. One reloading was required to shave the edge of the auto-pistol shooters.

9.2 It Makes You Think

Note that each course adds up to more than six shots. You aren't told how to fire it. You have to think for yourself. And you'd better learn to count your shots so that you don't lose time when the hammer clicks to remind you that your gun is empty. Each course is individually timed. Your raw score, less penalty points for misses and other transgressions, is divided by the time it took you to complete the course. A heavy caliber scores higher

A challenging practical pistol course can be constructed with a minimum of makeshift junk; a sheet and 2x4's make a wall, sawhorses a tunnel. Nothing fancy, but it does the trick.

than the "light" .38 Special. So the emphasis is on accuracy, speed, and power—all desirable when you face a threat on the street.

If you ride in a cruiser all day, or sit at a desk, you'll know that you toned up some muscles after firing an IPSC match. It was three days later before I could walk without a limp.

What did I gain? *Confidence!*

You learn that you can think through a challenging situation, fire effectively in a minimum of time, and do better the next time because your muscles are better prepared.

And it was fun.

Any time you find something that sharpens your skills and you have a ball doing it, it's worth a try.

10

Keep Control of Your Gun

Think back. How many of your schoolmates were football stars? How many climbed the rope without hesitation on their first try? How many could do a hundred pushups without puffing? Not many.

I was no shining example in "phys ed" either, so I worried. Suppose some wiry wrongdoer wrestled me for my gun?

That's a concern of anyone who is armed. According to FBI Uniform Crime Reports, 106 officers were killed in 1979, 17 with their own guns. In 1977, 10 percent of the officers killed were killed with their own guns; in 1978, 15 percent; in 1979, 16 percent. It's a growing threat.

In Kansas City, Missouri, from January 1975 through June 1976, there were nine cases of officers disarmed. One was killed. One was shot in the leg. One was brutally beaten by an assailant who later killed a cab driver with the officer's revolver.

"We evaluated and classified every case we could get a history on to determine the causes and develop a training program to respond to the most frequent circumstances," James Lindell said.

Lindell is Physical Training Supervisor for the KC Police. He's a martial arts expert, lanky and lithe; his graying hair belies what he can do to you with just his hands and feet. He is expert enough to know that not all men behind the badge have the physique or motivation to become Black Belts.

10.1 How Guns Are Grabbed

The Administrative Analysis Division of the KCPD identified a number of common circumstances in gun-grab cases. They identified how guns are grabbed. Experimenting with different martial arts and by trial and error, Lindell developed a simplified system aimed at defending the officer's revolver. Personal defense is a natural consequence.

In 1976, the KCPD adopted Lindell's initial *Revolver Retention* system; it has been evolving and improving ever since. To date, in some 30 cases of disarming attempts, not one was successful.

Lindell conducted a Justice System Training Association regional instructor training seminar at the Smith & Wesson Academy in 1981. I attended.

Most of the police officers in the class were young, younger than my then-54 years, that is. They were athletic, compared with my paunch. But ever the gentleman, Lindell didn't look at me when he said, "Martial arts aren't the sole answer, but these principles can be applied to procedures that the *average* officer can easily do."

He must have been right. I passed the course.

10.2 The Lindell System

We won't try to summarize Lindell's entire training manual. You can get a copy from Odin Press, Box 11688, Kansas City, MO, 64138. It should be part of all police firearms training.

10.2.1 Three Simple Steps

Without disclosing any secrets, the *Handgun Retention* course boils down to three simple steps: (1) Secure the gun, (2) Position, and (3) Release.

The assailant is intent on grabbing your gun. That's the target. Not you. So the first thing is to secure the gun in the holster with one hand as you position yourself in a way that provides protection, and gives the leverage that is more than the attacker can resist.

Keeping it simple, Lindell applies just five techniques that respond to virtually all the possible attempts to grab a holstered gun. If your gun is drawn, there are just four techniques you need to know, and they are virtually sure to keep control of your gun in your hands. Even if the assailant

Handgun retention is a major part of firearms training. Here, James Lindell of the Kansas City (Missouri) Police Department demonstrates how easy it is to take a gun away from an aggressor who is within grabbing distance.

has the drop on you, or gets your gun out of the holster, there are three techniques that, in the twinkling of an eye, will turn the tables.

10.2.2 Anyone Can Do It

These simple three-step procedures use wristlocks (jujitsu), blocks (karate), and throws (judo). But you don't need to know the physics of body mechanics, leverage, and nerves to apply these principles. The secret is first learning the fundamentals—properly. Then practice, practice, practice. It's like drawing your revolver. With practice, when the occasion arises, your response just happens, without conscious thought.

One of Lindell's students tells the story, "I felt the grab on my gun and the next thing I knew, the guy was on the ground and my gun was in my hand aimed right at his temple."

There are other effective systems developed and taught by well-known instructors. But judging by what I've read by the pundits of police survival, Lindell's method is the simplest and most easily done by the cruiser or desk-bound patrolman who does not enjoy working out in the gym every day.

That suits me to a tee.

11

Secrets of Good Shooting

"Boy! If only I had a gussied-up gun like that guy's got, I'd shoot better scores, too."

To some extent, that sentiment has probably crossed your mind. And there is reason why the serious competitive shooter does different things to his gun. But not necessarily the reasons you think.

"What difference the gun makes" sounded like an intriguing experiment that could lead to findings of interest to you. So, we put together a group of guns and put shooters of varying skill levels through comparative courses of fire.

11.1 What Difference a Gun Makes

A serious competitive Combat and IPSC shooter, Capt. Dwight Brouillard of the Hampden County (Massachusetts) Sheriff's Department joined me for a session at the Agawam Pistol Club range. We each shot a group of three Smiths, a four-inch K frame revolver, a four-inch L frame, and a six-inch L frame. The L frame is a revolver that comes from the factory designed much like the guns used by top Police Combat competitors. To introduce greater difficulty, we shot all standing point-shoulder, 12 shots

80

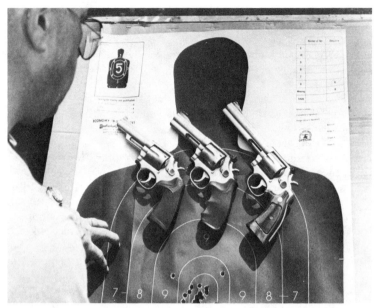

Three guns used in our informal evaluation proved that *you* are more important than the custom designs used by many target shooters. Capt. Dwight Brouillard of the Hampden County (Massachusetts) Sheriff's Department did better with his own four-inch L frame, and I did almost as well with my own four-inch K frame as I did with the six-incher.

at 7 yards, 6 at 15, and 12 at 25, all on the NRA B-27 target with scoring rings.

Over this course, Brouillard scored 283 x 300 with the K frame, then a 295 with the six-inch L frame but, on the final round, he tallied 298 with the four-inch L frame. My scores were just as strange. With the four-inch L frame, my score was 279; with the six-inch L frame, it was 286. My final round was 285 with the four-inch K frame, my own "wearing" piece.

In an earlier session on the Connecticut State Police range, we had to use the training silhouettes, so the score is the K5 total.

Dan Mathena of the Canton (Connecticut) Police scored 22 with my well-used K frame, 20 with the four-inch L, and 23 with the six-inch L. Don Poist of the Bradley Airport Police blew the whole deal by scoring 22 with each of the three guns. My scores were 17 with the K, 16 with the four-inch L, and 20 with the six-incher.

Everyone agreed that my four-inch K and the six-inch L had been fired enough to "break them in." The four-inch L was fresh off the shelf, and still a bit stiff. That explains the better scores with the K, even though both officers liked the four-inch L best of all. They also agreed that the six-inch L frame was steadiest on target.

The Agawam Pistol Club held a "Street Survival" match, which involved firing from strange positions at multiple targets, against the clock. Purposely, I fired twice through the course, scoring 66 percent with my own four-inch K frame and 74 percent with the six-inch L frame.

Now, this is far from a controlled laboratory experiment, but it tells me two things loud and clear:

1. A well-balanced revolver, like the L frame, fires tighter groups; the longer sight radius of the six-inch barrel is also a group-tightener for the target shooter, but awkward when sitting in a patrol car.

2. The most important factor is the shooter's experience with whatever revolver he uses.

One might expect scores to be higher with the six-inch barrel L frame revolver, as our shooting proved. With a longer sight radius and full-length barrel shroud, the gun hangs on target steadier. I would have expected to do better with the four-inch L but, in the first session, it was still too fresh. In the second session, we used Dwight's own personal four-inch L frame. Its action was smooth, but he had special target sights. My ancient eyes could not center his black front post as well as the red ramp front on the gun I had.

So, Dwight scored better with his own gun, three points better than his score with the six-incher. And my personal gun, for me, scored within a point of my performance with the six.

This tells me that a shooter will score better with a gun he knows intimately. It is also apparent that any individual will find features and accouterments that suit him better than others.

11.2 Competition Is Something Else

A serious competitive shooter makes choices because of the volume of shooting he does. Grips, for example. Fitted grips help him to stand the gaff. In our shooting tests, Dwight and I swapped our own set of grips onto each gun we fired, to be sure that each gun felt the same.

A revolver that has been "broken in" by a lot of shooting is naturally going to perform better for you. But not just because you've "smoothed up" the action. It's because *you* have practiced and know the gun better. The weight of the trigger pull doesn't matter if you are accustomed to it. The *smoothness* of the pull is the more important factor. I once shot a revolver in several competitions before I discovered the trigger pull was heavier than necessary. But it was smooth, so my scores were acceptable.

So why does the serious competitor go to such lengths to tailor his gun?

He uses special sights, special grips, anything he can find to "fine-tune" his performance and endure repetitive firing. If your sight picture is sharp, the fuller target front sight holds sighting error to a minimum. My sights aren't so sharp, so the latitude of combat sights helps me—but I probably won't win the Nationals, either.

11.3 Practical Skills Are Critical

On the street, you're not concerned with your shot being an "X" instead of just a "10." You *are* concerned that it be in the "K" zone. You can learn to perform that well with your duty gun, whatever it is.

When you have a choice of guns, certain ones will help you to perform better than others. Only your own practice on the range will tell you which gun feels right, for you.

12

Leather Makes a Difference

Like the cowboy with the ubiquitous Winchester, the policeman always has his sidearm. But that isn't the only similarity.

Both cowboy and cop depend not upon the gun itself for survival, but upon their individual ability to use that gun. Thus, confidence is the factor that can make the difference between proper or improper use. If you are confident, you can take the time to make the proper decision. If you are confident in your leather, for example, you'll know that you will have the gun when you need it.

Pictures in history books show some rather simple designs for holsters worn by settlers. They were simply a means of toting the gun comfortably, with no thought to providing a function. But pictures of the early gunfighters show different kinds of holsters. These were ones that not only carried the gun but also had to provide easy access so that the gun could be brought into play – quickly.

There are similar differences among holsters manufactured today. Some inexpensive models do nothing more than tote the gun. The models you are interested in are probably not inexpensive, but they are designed to do more. If you have to buy your own holster, remember how important it is when you evaluate the price tag.

12.1 Gun Rig Is More than a Holster

Just because we're talking about "holsters," don't forget that there's a belt involved, too. The Western rig obviously includes a cartridge belt. Your police holster goes on a Sam Browne belt. Too seldom do you hear it said, "The holster depends upon the belt it's on." Some holster designs won't work without a firm foundation. Some are just uncomfortable if the fit of holster to belt is improper. We'll say more about that later, but just keep in mind that your leather rig includes a holster *and* a belt.

The cowboy slung his six-gun low on his hip, with the grip cocked out into thin air where anyone could grab it. How many cops have you seen doing the same?

12.2 Security Holsters

Many departments have gone to a "security" type of holster that resists a gun grab by an assailant. But they met resistance from the officers who had to wear them. It's a natural reaction for one who thinks a security holster is going to restrict his own access to his gun.

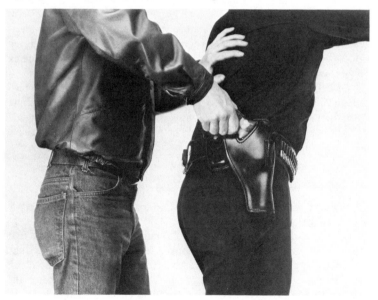

With a good security-style holster, it is difficult for a gun grabber to get your gun out of its holster. But don't depend on technology, which is only an aid, not a solution. *Bill Hill Photo.*

The feeling of "too much" security may be enhanced by your first feeble efforts to draw from a holster of this type.

Any holster that holds your gun differently than its predecessor takes some getting used to. You wouldn't step from a police cruiser into a Corvette without noticing differences. But once you become accustomed to those differences and polish your technique, the feeling changes.

Hartford, Connecticut, was one of the first cities to adopt a security holster because, as police Sgt. Bill O'Brien told me, "On the street, you're a big man in the gang if you grab a cop's gun." A natural reluctance to change was seen among the troops.

Reluctance disappeared after a rock concert. "For the first time, the cops had both hands free to defend themselves. Before, they had to use one hand to protect their guns," O'Brien explained. "I can say without fear of exaggeration that at least 30 guys have been saved by the security holster over the past two years."

12.3 Security Not Sure

There was one case of a successful gun grab, but the cop collared the grabber.

A left-handed officer was standing at the counter in the store interviewing the clerk when he felt the grab on his left-side holster. O'Brien deduces that the officer turned to his left, toward the grabber, thus forcing the gun out of the holster in the way it was intended to be drawn.

Object lessons: turn away from a gun grabber so that the gun is forced back under the trigger guard hood. Also, realize that no product is absolute. If a holster were absolutely secure, how could you draw your own gun?

Any security holster requires that you perfect your technique, practice your draw. So don't knock it if you haven't tried it.

12.4 Appearance Is a Factor

My duty leather has evolved into a comfortable rig that protects my gun better than I can.

When Smith & Wesson's Concealed Thumb Break Duty holster first came out, one went on my belt and it looked sexy. The butt of the gun stuck out, where it was readily accessible. I used that rig in conducting handgun retention classes and, surprisingly, others found it difficult to snatch the gun from that exposed position even before I applied retention techniques.

But at roll call one evening, the shift commander was our firearms instructor. He took one look at my rig and said, "Aha, a suicide special."

"Oh, this is my rig for combat shooting," I replied, almost truthfully. But I quickly sprung for another belt for a competition rig and a new B30

Security holster went onto the duty belt. Frankly, those early model security holsters conflicted with that little bit of "cowboy" in all of us. I thought they looked bulky. The idea was good, but I'm as reluctant to change as the next man. That is, I was until I practiced with this new model.

Now my opinion is that it looks good on the hip. But, more importantly, it keeps the gun where it belongs, even under adverse conditions. Yet I can get the gun out as smoothly and quickly as with any other holster. I'm in good company. Four major departments in my area have standardized on this security holster.

And that Shift Commander thinks I'm safe on the street, now.

12.5 Public Image Affected

This type of security holster covers the gun, which is protected from the elements. Only the grip sticks out where you can grab it quickly. A front leaf spring pushes the gun back so that the trigger guard rides back and under a reinforced hood. There's no way a gun grabber can twist or yank the gun out of the holster, except in the manner it was intended to be drawn.

The early models of security holsters took some training to develop a smooth draw. Some relied on gimmicks, release latches that sometimes let go when you least expected it. That can be embarrassing. Don't rely on gimmicks. With a well-designed model, it doesn't take long to get used to. Just one session on the range should do the trick. With a smooth circular motion draw raking the gun forward, the gun comes out of this security holster as easily as from a Jordan-style combat holster.

The old compromise between safety and speed no longer is a problem.

There is even an advantage for your department's public image. In many duty holsters, the butt of the gun is canted away from the body so that it sticks out like the cowboy's .45 single-action. This may look macho as the officer swaggers down the street with the sun dancing off the stainless steel revolver. But it doesn't help your image among your fellow citizens.

And it may even entice a grabber.

The newer security holsters tuck the gun closer to the body. The grip is still clear for a quick draw, but the gun itself is unobtrusive. My black Pachmayr "Gripper" or Hogue grips are the same color as the holster. The appearance of this rig could hardly offend anyone, much less be "threatening."

Yet the gun is as accessible to me as it was in my former Thumb Break Duty holster. And that's top priority in my book.

If you have a choice in your leather, a good security holster is as worthy an investment as a "bulletproof" vest. It can help insure that your gun will be where you expect it to be, when you need it most.

13

How to Live with
Your Duty Gun and Love It

If you wear an off-duty gun different from your duty gun, some departments require that you qualify with it. That's a good idea. If that different gun is a back-up piece, you qualify with that, too. But if you wear a four-inch barrel revolver on duty, why in the world do you need a different gun to wear off duty?

There are some fundamentals you should keep in mind.

13.1 Habit Is Hard to Break

As already stated, the statistical average fire fight sees some 2.3 shots expended in something like 2.7 seconds. If you want a 14-shot auto for off duty, fine—if that is your duty gun. But what if your duty gun is a revolver? Are you going to remember the different handling and functioning characteristics of the auto when you need to react instinctively?

13.2 Performance Is No Compromise

The whole world seems to wear a two-inch barrel revolver with civilian clothes. But look at ballistics. Take the .38 Special + P, 125-grain JHP load.

Muzzle velocity from a six-inch barrel revolver is 1,143 fps (feet per second). From a four-inch barrel it's 1,040 fps. That's a reduction of only nine percent. But when you drop to a two-inch barrel, muzzle velocity decreases to 897 fps, a reduction of an additional 14 percent. You lose more by shortening the barrel from four to two inches than you do from six to four.

"But that little snubby tucks handily away, and you hardly know it's there," one friend argued.

"Yeah," I counter, "and I feel as if it's continually falling out because there's no barrel below the belt."

Another friend, Capt. Robert K. Lindsey of the Jefferson Parish Sheriff's Department in Louisiana, wears a Model 19 with six-inch barrel, on duty, off duty, in sport clothes or business suit. He's a tall guy. But he demonstrates the point I want to make: *You can wear whatever gun you want to wear, comfortably and conveniently, provided you rig it right.* My tall friend can wear his six-incher. It would give a short-waisted fellow like me a problem. Most cops wear a four-inch revolver on duty, and I contend that you can wear that same four-inch revolver off duty with as much *savoir faire* as a detective wears his snubby status symbol.

Now, I'm not talking about wearing a backup gun. I've become a believer in the two-inch, .38 Special, loaded with Federal's Chief's Special loads in that funny little Pop Up holster that tucks under your waistband. I wore it all one summer and no one detected it. The first week I wore an ankle holster, my wife asked, "What's wrong with your foot?"

Bob Lindsey wears his six-incher in a pancake-style hip holster, right near the same place where his duty holster rides. My four-inch Model 66 rides in a right hip, forward tilt pancake-style holster, and I'll swear it's more comfortable than a snubby. As I said, I feel as if the snubby is insecure.

The FBI gave a lot of thought and consideration before they came up with the now traditional right hip, FBI tilt mode of wearing a weapon.

Gun, holster, and belt. Those are the three elements of your off-duty rig; don't skimp on any one.

GUN. Let's say a four-inch barrel revolver, your duty gun. You are familiar with it. You've practiced with it. You handle it instinctively. You point it naturally. It hits what you point it at. It has enough barrel to be seen in your peripheral vision when you shoot from the hip. Why would you want something different?

HOLSTER. Obviously, I've led you to the hugger or pancake-style so that it's in the same place you would instinctively reach for your duty gun. But that holster won't act right if you put it on a decorative waist strap.

BELT. It deserves more credit than it gets. The holster and belt have to fit together. The slots in my holster are cut to fit a 1¾-inch belt. That

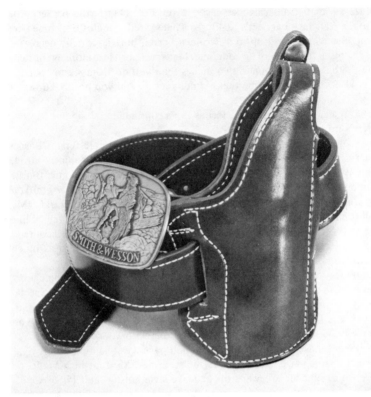

The holster is only part of the equipment that properly rigs a gun for off-duty carry. The belt is critical, too. Proper fit means that the entire rig is comfortable, and proper design means that it is hardly noticeable. *Lloyd Burnham Photo.*

holster, on a lined 1¾-inch belt, rides snugly without any flop. It's comfortable. On a thin, cheap 1¼-inch belt, it rides less firmly. The grip of the gun slaps my side and it quickly becomes uncomfortable.

The rig for your duty gun off duty consists of a holster *and a belt*. If you depend on that rig to protect your life, you don't want any part of it to be supplied by the lowest bidder.

14

Your Off-Duty Gun

Policemen have long used a more compact sidearm for off-duty carry. Too many own small pocket autos, or small snub nose revolvers. The case has already been made that you're better off wearing your duty gun off duty. You don't *need* a second gun. But, if you're going to be obstinate and insist on wearing some petite pistol in civilian clothes, I'd be derelict in my duty if I didn't raise some important points.

An off-duty gun is selected for comfort and convenience of carry. But did you stop to think that you may need to depend on it as much as you do your service revolver? Where does that leave your puny pocket pistols?

New York City Police did an analysis of 6,000 officer-involved shootings. It was found that the service revolver was used in 60 percent of the incidents. In 35 percent of the gunfights a small revolver was the weapon used. But the study does not identify the gun or its caliber. In the remaining five percent, the weapon was another type of handgun, or a shotgun.

14.1 Second Gun Liability

Your department has trained you with your service revolver. If it is misused, abused, or becomes the object of a lawsuit, the department is in your corner. If your off-duty gun is your own, one the department doesn't know about, watch out.

Paul Patti wrote in *Police Marksman* magazine of the concerns over a second gun. He checked with his local state's attorneys, and none saw any liability beyond what might be incurred with a duty gun, if misused. I've found complete agreement, however, on certain important legal points: the lack of a policy may well incur liability, the lack of training may well incur liability, and inadequate training may well incur liability.

If you wear a sidearm different from your duty gun, you'd better have qualified with it under your department instructor. Otherwise, you could find yourself hanging alone on the hook of liability.

14.2 Same Type Important

What type should your second gun be? Obviously, it should function the same as the duty gun you are trained with. It could cost critical time

Off-duty guns may have to be a compromise to achieve comfort. The "world's best backup gun," the two-inch snubby, is easier to handle with combat grips. *Lloyd Burnham Photo.*

to change your habits in the heat of a confrontation. If you have practiced most with your duty gun, why not rig it for off-duty carry? If your duty gun is a four-inch revolver, you can wear it as comfortably as the snubby status symbol usually worn as an off-duty gun.

There are times when it is more convenient to wear a compact pistol. For those times, however, you still must make a sensible choice. If your duty gun is a four-inch .38 Special revolver, the small frame .38 Special two-incher isn't a bad choice—with the proper ammunition. If you wear a .357 Magnum revolver, a three-inch, round butt Magnum is a comfortable gun to carry. If you are armed with a high magazine capacity auto-pistol, there are compact companion pieces on the market.

What caliber should the second gun be? If it uses issue ammunition, you don't have to buy a different caliber cartridge. Your partner has a ready supply should you need it. And heaven forbid that you should ever get your ammo mixed in with department ammo when you are trying to reload in a hurry.

If your duty gun is an auto, one of the compact 9mm's is a good choice. Manufacturers include Smith & Wesson, Colt, Beretta, Heckler & Koch, Steyr, and Iver Johnson. *Smith & Wesson Photo.*

14.3 Subcalibers Inadequate

In a study done with the help of the Los Angeles and San Francisco police departments of shootings involving "subcaliber" guns, Richard Seldeen found that in some 300 cases the deceased was ambulatory and coherent for 10 to 60 seconds, even when the heart itself was struck, unless the bullet struck the central nervous system directly. Even with multiple, potentially lethal wounds, the aggressor would be able to return fire.

He defines "subcaliber" as .22 or .25 caliber.

Tony Lesce points out in an article he wrote in *Police Marksman* that "placement" of a shot is more important than "power" of the shot. A New York City report holds this finding consistent with calibers ranging from .22 Long Rifle to .44 Magnum.

Not many of us can pick which shirt button to hit, so don't handicap yourself with some pip-squeak just because it's "convenient."

15

The Backup Gun
Needs Thought

Hardly an issue of a police publication goes by that someone doesn't write
about the "second" gun that seems to be growing in popularity. I've read
articles about types, calibers, liability, and tactics. The question has long
since been decided; a backup gun could be the most important number in
your arsenal. We've all read of cases where an officer's life was saved because
of the backup gun that the gang of hoods didn't know he had. And that's
really the critical element — *the element of surprise.*

15.1 Surprise Is the Advantage

The uniformed officer is decked out with more gear than is comfortable
to carry. Your sidearm sticks out like a bastion of power. Everyone knows
you have it. A "gentleman" becomes a big man on the street if he takes it
away from you. Security holsters help, but guns have been grabbed after
they're out of the holster. Then where's the poor cop?

In one case I read, the policeman found himself staring down the barrel of his own gun. The felon thought he was master of the situation and
gave the officer that critical second of inattention in which to react — with

his backup gun. Because the crook thought he had disarmed the officer, he was careless. The officer had the element of surprise to his advantage.

Paul Patti, the *Police Marksman* writer, told the story of two West Palm Beach, Florida, officers who stopped to check a man resembling the description of an armed robbery suspect. They frisked him and found him unarmed. While putting the man in the patrol car, the suspect disarmed one officer and wounded him with his own gun. Before the suspect could turn and shoot the second officer, the wounded officer shot and killed the man with his concealed second handgun.

This means that your backup gun must not only be convenient to carry, but it must also be accessible — and it must be *effective*. When you call on a backup gun, you're already in deep trouble. Frankly, I think anything less than a four-inch .357 Magnum is not effective enough. But, I must admit, it isn't the most convenient thing to hide. So the compromise begins.

Both Paul Patti and Tony Lesce agree on what a police department policy on backup guns should include. The second gun and its holster should be a high quality, recognized brand. It should use department-issue ammunition and be listed with and inspected by the department armorer. It should be carried concealed, and the officer must qualify with whatever gun he wears.

15.2 Types of Backup Guns

There are hideaway guns designed especially for backup use. They are convenient but limit the number of shots available. The .380 autos give you six shots or more but in a caliber even less effective than the .38 Special. I own two palm-size .380 autos. They are little more than an annoyance with the usual full metal case (FMC) bullets. With the 84-grain jacketed hollow point (JHP) load they're almost adequate.

That brings us back to what I consider the world's most popular backup gun: the two-inch barrel, .38 Special revolver.

The compact snubby is convenient. The proper choice of ammunition makes it effective. But what about accessibility? That means not only where you can grab it in a hurry but also that it stays in your hand when it reaches firing position. You have to give a lot of thought as to *where* you carry a backup gun. Remember, it must be hidden to keep that element of surprise, yet be readily available when you need it.

15.3 Hideaway Holsters

Hideaway holsters are largely a matter of personal choice. There are styles designed to wear on the leg or ankle, forearm, armpit, small of the

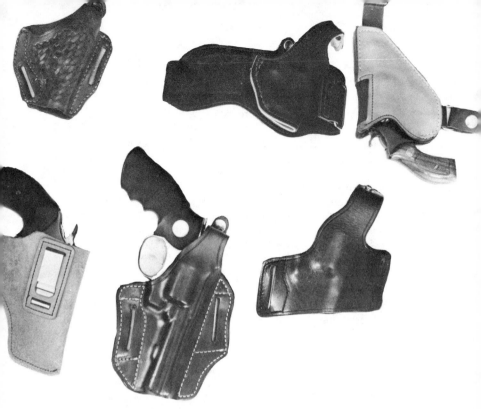

Hideaway holsters are made in many styles and types because people and their clothes are different. What's best for you is largely a personal choice. These holsters are representative: Top, from left, hugger, ankle holster, and upside-down shoulder holster. Bottom, from left, inside-the-waistband type, slimline, and revolver belt strap.

back, even down inside the waistband of your trousers. The choice is governed by how you dress, the cut of your clothes, and the shape of your body. That's why there are so many different kinds of hideaway holsters. But whatever your choice, it must hold the gun securely even when you run or scuffle. Practice drawing from it, so that you habitually reach for the right spot—without thinking.

15.4 Grip Important

To make these guns compact, everyone hedges on the grip. It usually is rounded, shorter than the one on your duty gun. My .380's must be held with two fingers, rather than three. The snub nose revolver uses as unobtrusive a grip as possible to make it easy to hide. My hands are of medium size. Most service grips are too small; most target grips are too big. But I've paid attention to grips ever since I saw a student on the range grab for a snubby. He didn't close his hand fast enough. The revolver rolled out of his grasp and went sailing across the range.

Combat-style grips serve a critical purpose. When you hastily grab for that snubby backup, it will stay in your hand. When the gun recoils, it has a firm foundation. If an assailant tries to snatch it away, you've got something to hold on to. And they are still reasonably convenient to hide.

You may never need a backup gun. But there were 59,031 reported assaults on officers, according to the FBI Uniform Crime Report for 1979; about 9.4 percent were committed with a blunt instrument, 5.5 percent with a firearm, and 2.4 percent with an edged weapon. About 20 percent of the officers killed with firearms were killed with their own guns.

Convenience, accessibility, and effectiveness. Those are the things you must think about in deciding on your backup gun rig. No one answer is best for everyone. Making the right personal choice takes considerable thought.

Police officers who carry a backup gun consider it an insurance policy. They'd rather have it and not need it, than need it and not have it.

16

Throwaway Gun
Is a Trap for Cops

Our discussion about a second gun means one that serves *your* purpose, not something to thwart the legal process. Your backup gun should be listed with your armorer, and you should have qualified with it on the range, the same as with your duty gun. The second gun that's unlisted, unlicensed, and untraceable is a snake just waiting to bite you.

The idea should have died a timely death a long time ago. I thought it had. But an officer told me that he has a friend who carries a "Saturday Night Special" just for that purpose. He said that if he had to shoot a suspect and later found him unarmed, he would press his throwaway into the dirtbag's fingers. That may sound like a way to avoid responsibility for a wrong judgment; but think again.

Massad Ayoob addressed this subject in an article he wrote for *Police Product News*. It's the best treatise on the subject I've ever read. Ayoob is a training Sergeant for a New Hampshire police department and runs the Lethal Force Institute in that state. He has spent several years in law enforcement. Ayoob has visited precincts, talked with street cops, and reported on conditions in some of the most strenuous turfs in the country, including New York's "Fort Apache." His qualifications for talking about the throwaway gun are far better than mine.

"On special assignments like a stakeout or a buy, I've had as many as five firearms on me or within easy reach," Ayoob explains. "For the record, every one of those guns was signed out to me."

He explains that the elements of premeditated murder include malice, forethought, and intentionally altering the evidence. If a cop carries an untraceable, printless firearm to plant on a guy that is mistakenly blown away, all those elements are present. Try explaining that in court.

The American criminal justice system is based on the "doctrine of the reasonable man." The criterion: "Would a reasonable man have done what you did?" If so, you are much better off in court than if you had dropped a throwaway gun. You can bet that public pressure will demand a thorough and intensive investigation of the incident.

Do you really think you could keep the throwaway a secret?

If your action is in response to a threat you perceive from a subject who has the opportunity, capability, and makes a move that telegraphs this intent to put you in jeopardy, your action should be upheld whether the guy actually had a gun. I've seen a number of such cases in my local area in recent years, and every one was decided in favor of the officer.

Ayoob cites eight ways a throwaway gun can trap you:

1. That throwaway came from somewhere. You confiscated it, bought it from a shady character, inherited it from your grandfather, or received it as a gift from a close friend. There is someone, somewhere, who can connect that gun to you — in court.

2. If the throwaway is truly untraceable to you, you still don't know where the gun was or what it did. Suppose you total your cruiser some icy night and the ambulance rushes you to the emergency room. Your personal effects are turned over to your Sergeant; included are your service revolver and that off-brand .32. Sarge is curious. He runs it through NCIC (National Crime Information Center) and gets a hit. It now goes to the ballistics lab, where they match it with a bullet recovered in the fatal shooting of a dope dealer in an adjacent city. Try explaining that one.

3. You had a friendly dispatcher run the gun through and it came back negative. Years later you drop it in a dead guy's hand. This time the gun is run through NCIC or the BATF (Bureau of Alcohol, Tobacco and Firearms) computer bank and it comes back that your friend's department queried that gun. They come down on your friend, now your *ex*-friend.

4. Even the most cautious cop with a drop gun dresses in the locker room or bedroom at home. A partner or wife has probably picked up on the fact that you've got it. Could you murder your ex-partner or ex-wife to silence them before the murder trial?

5. You'd probably have to murder the victim. In three out of four police shootings, Ayoob says, the victim is only wounded. He survives. If you plant

a piece on him, he'll remember. When you pulled the trigger the first time, you did it under reasonable fear and in good faith. If you pull the trigger later, it's cold-blooded murder.

6. The aftermath of a good faith shooting is hectic. You call for backup, an ambulance. It may take a while before you realize the guy wasn't packing a gun. By then, you're swarmed with witnesses. How can you drop a throwaway without being noticed?

7. Whether you have faith in the polygraph or not, you just may face one. When the question is asked, "Did you plant the weapon on the dead suspect?", do you think you can keep that needle from jumping?

8. Even if you give up the idea of a drop gun after others know you once carried one, you're branded for life. Years later, you pull over a guy who points a .38 at you and you blow him away. His gun comes back as one of those "untraceable" ones and everyone thinks it was yours.

Let's close this subject forever. Drop guns get you into more trouble than they get you out of, and could even give you free room and board for life where your wife can visit you once each month.

17

Ammunition Makes
Your Gun Work

A hammer is little good without a nail. A book is only paper without the ink to make words on it. A computer is only an unfunctioning electronic gadget without its software. Likewise, your gun is only a conglomerate of metal and other parts until you mate it with the expendable items it uses to perform its function. The gun is only a tool.

17.1 History

The Chinese invented the stuff that explodes inside the firecracker. The mixture of materials that make up black powder provide a simple product that is a fun celebration — until you add the metal that harnesses the power potential of the expanding gases that result from the burning of that powder. At first, it was a simple pipe with a closed end. You could put powder in it from the muzzle, add a wad to contain the expanding gases, then top it off with a bunch of junk or a ball that those gases would expel with great force. This was the hand cannon, the original firearm. There was a little hole toward the rear through which a spark could ignite the powder charge. The principle remained the same through the arquebus, snaphaunce, matchlock, flintlock, and percussion lock guns down through history.

Then some fellow got the idea of packaging pre-measured portions of all these components in a combustible container. This led to the development of the first breechloading firearm. To make a long story short, the paper cartridge was quickly replaced with the brass cartridge case into which a priming compound was put under a pin, or inside the crushable rim, and finally into a separate little cup that fits into a receptacle in the base of the case. Powder was measured into the brass case and the bullet crimped into the open end to close it.

17.2 Ammunition Parts

The two preceding paragraphs quickly summarize what others have spent volumes to explain, but we now know that a cartridge consists of four parts: the case, primer, powder, and bullet. That's all we really need to know.

There are different size primers for different type cartridges: larger for large cartridges and smaller for small cartridges, generally.

There are different type powders for different type cartridges. Some powders burn quickly; they're used in pistol calibers, because of their relatively short barrels. Other powders burn slower; they're used in rifle cartridges, with their longer barrels. Other powders are designed for shotshells.

Modern smokeless powder does not explode. It burns, rapidly. Pull the bullet out of a .22 cartridge and spill it into an ashtray. Touch a match to it and it only burns, no bang. What makes it powerful is that the product of that burning is a lot of gas that has to go somewhere. If it is contained in your stomach, you know where it goes. If it is constrained inside the cartridge case in the chamber of a firearm, it is going to push through the path

Pulling apart an actual cartridge seemed the best way to illustrate that it's made up of four major parts, from left: primer, case, powder, and bullet.

All the bullets in this photo are essentially the same caliber. But they're all different in design. From left, 9mm 115-grain, JHP; .38 Special 125-grain, JHP; .357 Magnum 158-grain, SWCHP; .38 Special 158-grain, JHP; and .38 Special 158-grain, RN Nyclad.

of least resistance — the bullet moves before anything else. The rapidly expanding gases push it through the bore, and send it on its way.

There are different types of bullets, too, and this does concern you. Most of the early cartridges were loaded with simple round nose lead bullets. But even in frontier days, the .45 Colt Peacemaker used a bullet with a flat nose. Those using them readily saw that a flat-nosed bullet slapped harder than a round nose bullet.

17.3 Bullet Design Affects Performance

Nowadays, bullet design is more scientific. Hollow points are designed to make the bullet upset more easily. Bullet jackets are necessary for the high temperatures at which modern powders burn and high velocities at which the bullets move. The alloy of the lead used to make the bullet differs, depending upon the velocity at which it is likely to be driven. Thus, a particular bullet marked for .38 Special is *not* the same as an identical bullet marked for .357 Magnum. The alloy is different.

The *shape* of the bullet has a lot to do with how it flies through the air and how it acts when it hits something. Wadcutters are not perfectly flat on the point, but they do have a wide shoulder that cuts a clean hole in a paper target. Other target bullets, with a point to provide needed weight, also have sharp paper-cutting shoulders.

I bring all this up simply so that you will understand there are differences in ammunition and a wide variety of loads that you can use in your particular gun, whatever it is.

18

Ammunition Makes
the Gun a 'Team'

Talk about guns all you will, but that gun is not as good as a baton without the ammunition that makes it work. You can't say one gun is more "effective" than another gun — within the caliber, of course — because performance is more a result of ammunition design than gun design.

18.1 Ammo to Suit the Purpose

That oversimplification makes the point that you may not have a choice in the gun you wear. But you can argue for a more "effective" choice in the ammunition you are allowed to use. Department regulations *can* be changed.

Since 1975, there has been a general trend to the .357 Magnum cartridge over the .38 Special, especially where most patrol activities are on main highways. I've heard it said by some municipal police officials, "We don't want the penetration of a Magnum round because of our urban situation." Then they require their cops to carry 158-grain round nose bullets in their .38 Specials. These bullets penetrate far more than the light jacketed hollow point (JHP) bullet from a .357 Magnum and can ricochet around a crowd of innocent bystanders or pass through an apartment wall into an adjacent room. The truth probably is that a department that owns hundreds of perfectly usable .38 Special revolvers isn't going to change quickly, for obvious reasons.

Suppose you're equipped with a four-inch, .38 Special. The choice of ammunition does make a difference. The lighter JHP bullet is a "controlled expansion" bullet, designed to mushroom more quickly in the target and *stop*. The bullet is supposed to expend its kinetic energy within the target more effectively. The round nose bullet holds together better. Unless it hits bone, it could pass right through the target, bounce off a wall, and end up just about anywhere.

Most gun experts agree that the .38 Special is a marginal load for law enforcement use. The 158-grain round nose lead bullet is inadequate, incapable of stopping a rabid dog, much less a crazed criminal. Most police loads are designed to be fired from a revolver with at least a four-inch barrel. The .38 Special +P load with a 125-grain JHP bullet is much more effective than the round nose lead because of its bullet design and velocity. But the hard jacket means you really can't get all that the bullet has to offer

Firearms Instructor Stanley Solek of the Berlin (Connecticut) Police Department helped to demonstrate the importance of selecting the right load for your gun. With his two-inch "Chief's Special," he shot water-filled cans with different bullets, to show the effectiveness of various weights and configurations.

These seamless aluminum cans show dramatically the difference between the impact of the .38 Special 158-grain round nose bullet, left, and the Federal "Chief's Special" 125-grain Nyclad hollow-point, right.

if you shoot it out of a shorter barrel. Makers of small frame snubbies tell you not to use +P loads as a steady diet.

An all-lead bullet can upset better than a jacketed bullet. But then you have the problems of leading, bore fouling, lubricant smoke, and even air pollution from lead oxides emitted by the hot gases that sear the base of the bullet.

18.2 Nyclad Bullets

The closing of indoor ranges because of air pollution led to the development of a Nylon-clad bullet that provides the advantages of a jacket to shield the lead from the burning powder gases, yet is soft enough that it makes the bullet act like all-lead. The result is the even, consistent expansion of an all-lead bullet, with all the advantages of a jacketed bullet.

Nyclad bullets, developed by Smith & Wesson, are now produced by Federal Cartridge Company; one particular load is still called "Chief's Special."

18.3 A Load for Snubbies

Because the short, two-inch barrel sacrifices so much of the ammunition's potential performance, as compared with longer barrels, my wife wouldn't let me put in print my opinion of snubbies as manstoppers. But this "Chief's Special" load changed my mind.

Clay is a good medium only to illustrate bullet cavity. The "Chief's Special" load, above, is compared with the service load, a 125-grain JHP + P, below.

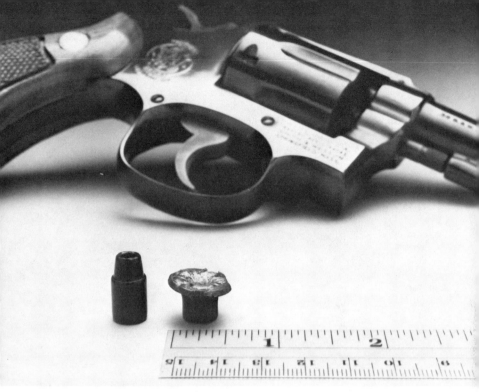

A recovered upset bullet from the "Chief's Special" load shows its performance from a two-inch barrel revolver. *Federal Cartridge Corp. Photo.*

Factory tests by Federal show that this 125-grain hollow point (HP) Nyclad load produces pressures below standard +P levels. It was designed for short barrel, alloy frame revolvers; yet, when fired from a two-inch barrel, the average muzzle velocity is 825 fps — less than five percent below the figure for the typical higher pressure +P load. Typical bullet expansion in ordnance gelatin at ten yards is .60 inches — a 25 percent increase over the average full load JHP +P.

You now have a wide range of choices for the fodder you feed whatever .38 Special you carry. It's worth the time and effort to try them all with a target that gives you an indication of their effect *on the target*. A gallon milk jug, or quart oil can filled with water, is one way to find out what loads are best.

18.4 Try It Yourself

I went to a range recently with Stanley Solek, a firearms instructor for the Berlin (Connecticut) Police to test this idea. From about 20 feet, the

158-grain round nose lead punched a hole in the oil can. The 125-grain Nyclad "Chief's Special" bullet bulged the top of the can and almost split the seam. On seamless aluminum beer cans, the difference was displayed more dramatically. The 158-grain round nose lead bullet split the far side of the can into an impressive exit. But the 125-grain Nyclad "Chief's Special" bullet blew out the middle of the can some two-thirds of the way around its circumference.

You, too, may be surprised with the results you find with the various choices of ammunition that are available. It's worth your time to visit a local range and do this experiment for your own self-assurance.

19

A Classic Controversy: Revolver vs. Automatic

Any gun writer worth his salt in the law enforcement field has written at least two articles during his career on whether the revolver or the semi-automatic pistol is the better police sidearm. It's one of those perennial subjects that changes a little each year, but always remains the same.

The question comes up again but, this time, for a different reason.

The bad guys who did the Brinks job in Nanuet, New York, were wearing soft body armor and were armed with 14-shot, 9mm pistols. They simply outgunned the two officers and guard armed with six-shot revolvers. This incident has spawned a number of cases where high-capacity magazine automatics have played a part. They are the favored sidearms of terrorist organizations, using the same ammunition as their submachine guns.

19.1 Self-Loaders Adopted

In the New York City area, freelance gun writer Dick Aarons reports that police are taking a hard look at the 9mm.

After losing a New Jersey State Trooper on a routine, rural traffic stop, the state's police fraternal organization demanded shotguns and 9mm autos for every trooper. The shotgun was granted immediately. The 9mm issue was evaluated by a police academy committee and the department adopted the Heckler & Koch Model P7, the "squeezecocker." The Connecticut State Police are armed with the Beretta Model 92SB. The Illinois State Police carry the S&W Model 439. All 9mm autos.

Police in Ridgefield, Connecticut switched to the Smith & Wesson Model 459. Det. Lt. Robert Brunnelle of that department refutes one of the old arguments against the self-loader. The revolver's operation, it is argued, is simpler and easier to master by those who couldn't care less about becoming expert marksmen. The automatic is more complex, features more details to remember, and requires more tender loving care. That's enough to convince the traditional revolver instructor that he was right all along.

But times are changing.

Even a guy who hates guns knows that his life may depend upon his skill with a gun. Training is improving. It's more comprehensive nowadays.

The Ridgefield (Connecticut) Police Department uses a high-capacity magazine pistol as its duty gun. Det. Lt. Robert Brunnelle retrained his department with surprisingly favorable results. Here, he discusses the new pistol with Sgt. William Green, right. *Dick Aarons Photo.*

Police comptrollers are more willing to invest public funds in training to protect the investments that jurisdictions have already made in each officer.

Nowadays, the bad guys are ganging up on the good guys.

Ridgefield switched because of the new threat of facing well-armed terrorists. Said Brunnelle: "It was 100 percent successful—more successful than we really thought it would be." Each officer was given two hours of classroom instruction. Range firing included 250 rounds in day qualification, and another 250 rounds at night. The surprising thing was that, on average, qualification scores showed a 20 percent improvement with the 9mm autos, compared with their former .357 Magnum revolvers.

19.2 Auto-Pistol Training Differs

Bob Hunt, currently the Director of the Smith & Wesson Academy, cautions that a few hours in class before the same old PPC is fired is not enough. It doesn't respond to the possibility of an officer facing an attacking force of well-armed terrorists after money bags in an armored truck.

Hunt developed two five-day training courses: *Auto Pistol I* and *Auto Pistol II*, that not only familiarize the student with the auto-pistol but trains him to employ the auto to its full potential.

The auto pistol has its advantages where basic firepower is a requirement. Learning to employ the potential of a 14-shot automatic is vastly different from training with a revolver. The situation shown here places paper "hostage" targets in front of the steel *Pepper Popper* bad guys.

"The officer with a six-shot revolver facing a half dozen terrorists must be cautious," Hunt says. "With a 15-shot auto and a couple of 20-round magazines on his belt, his attitude can be more aggressive. But he needs to develop the skills to effectively handle the increased potential of the auto-pistol. Training is the key."

Hunt teaches the Weaver stance with the auto because the shooter can recover more quickly. Shooting exercises involve multiple targets at different angles. Students learn to clear jams quickly. The possibility of a jam was one argument against the self-loader for police work. "But the chances of clearing a jam in an auto are far better than if the cylinder of your revolver jams," Hunt says.

In the *Auto Pistol I* course, shooting exercises are quite different than the old PPC. In one, five "reactive" steel targets — that fall when they're hit — were set up over a space of some 15 feet. Four were tucked behind two paper target "hostages." The student walked up from the firing line toward a mailbox. On the whistle, he had to take out the "greatest threat" target, get behind cover, and then take out the four partly hidden targets. A shot on a steel plate stopped the clock.

Such a situation requires firepower and gives the automatic the advantage.

19.3 Choice Depends on Circumstance

"How often will I ever have to face such a situation?" There are parts of the country where it's quite likely that you may face such a situation. On the other hand, there are parts of the country where your best choice of sidearm is a six-inch barrel .41 Magnum revolver. And you know how many parts of the country are still making-do with a four-inch .38 Special.

I strive to be an impartial reporter. I wore a GI automatic in the USAF Air Police (before they started calling them Security Police), and a number of pocket automatics have been my convenient off-duty guns. My duty gun now is a four-inch Model 66 that doubles as my off-duty gun, so you can say that I'm a wheelgun man. But I have lived with an auto-pistol, so it's no stranger.

When it comes to the classic argument over the revolver vs. the self-loader for police work, the articles I've read usually end up middle-of-the-road. Either is good; both have advantages and disadvantages. That is still true.

Which gun is "better" than the other still, and always will, depend upon the criteria *you* set for the demands it must meet. I will say that re-evaluation of your situation, in light of changing challenges, is well worth-while; but only *you* can really answer the question.

20

9mm: Is It Enough?

With all that has been written on the subject, the question of which is the better police sidearm, revolver, or auto-pistol, is usually answered, "It depends." It depends upon the situation, circumstances, and inclination.

But little is said about the *ammunition*.

If you face a situation where terrorist attack is likely, the auto-pistol provides more firepower than the revolver. If you live in the boondocks with lions and bears, a revolver provides heavier calibers than the auto.

People have personal preferences. Many instructors, however, tell me it is easier to train a raw recruit with a revolver than it is with an auto. And the tactics applied with the high capacity magazine auto are quite different than with the revolver. You need a new training program if your department switches to the self-loader. If you grew up on wheelguns, it may be more trouble than it's worth to change old habits.

20.1 9mm Pistol Widely Used

We know of some 94 law enforcement agencies that are armed, in part or in total, with a self-loading sidearm. The state police of Illinois, New Jersey, and Connecticut are armed with 9mm pistols. Some use it only for special response teams, as does the FBI with its Model 459s. A number of municipal departments have decided they are vulnerable to paramilitary radicals and need more firepower for an effective response.

In New Jersey, 28 police departments use the auto-pistol. In Illinois, the total is 17, including about one-fifth of the Chicago Police Department. Also using the auto-pistol are some 14 agencies in Wisconsin, 12 in California, four in New York, three each in Ohio and Pennsylvania, two in Massachusetts, Connecticut, and Kansas and one each in Florida, Maryland, Louisiana, Missouri, Nevada, and Arizona.

All of these pistols are 9mm.

There are officers who prefer and use the trusty .45 Auto. There's no question that the .45 ACP cartridge is effective. It has been our military round for sidearms and submachine guns for a long time. But there is also no question that the .45 Auto is just too much gun for many of today's smaller-statured Centurions. You can carry more 9mm ammunition because it is compact. So, when a department evaluates a proposal to switch from a wheelgun to a self-loader, it is invariably the 9mm auto that is considered.

It is apparent that police departments are re-evaluating their armaments in light of the potential threats they face. Some are opting for pistols that permit a policeman to carry a box of ammo ready for instant use. With a number of the high capacity magazine 9mm autos, you carry 14 rounds plus one in the chamber. Add a pair of 20-round magazines and you've got 55 shots on your belt.

Like Nassau County, New York, some police departments decided that the revolver represented adequate defense, especially in view of the task of completely retraining a 3,600-man department.

20.2 Ammo Comparison

The other side of this equation is the ammunition. How does the 9mm compare with your previous service loads, .38 Special, or .357 Magnum?

A big advantage of the compact 9mm cartridge is that you can carry more rounds of 9mm in the same space and weight as you can either of the two popular revolver calibers. But shot-for-shot, is the 9mm capable of doing the job?

The 9mm Parabellum cartridge has been around for many years. It was adopted as the official sidearm cartridge by the German Navy in 1904, and by the German Army in 1908. Pistols chambered for this cartridge include the historically famous Luger and the Walther P-38.

As a rule, ballistic tables show the 9mm to be two-thirds of the way up the scale from the .38 Special toward the .357 Magnum. So it has con-

To illustrate the various size cartridges a policeman may use, from left: .380 Auto 85-grain, JHP; 9mm 115-grain, JHP; .38 "Chief's Special" 125-grain SWCHP Nyclad; .38 Special +P+ (U.S. Treasury Department load); .38 Special AP (armor-piercing, from World War II); .357 Magnum 125-grain, JHP; .45 Colt; and .45 ACP.

siderably more punch than the trusty old .38, and not quite the punch of the .357.

The cartridge is only a hair more than an inch long, and about the same diameter as your revolver cartridge. But its small size is deceiving. Its secret lies in its ability to handle higher pressures than either the .38 Special, or even the good old .45 Auto. Factory rounds of 9mm with a 115-grain "controlled expansion" (hollow point) bullet are clocked at 1,165 feet per second (fps), with 349 foot pounds of energy from a four-inch barrel. The .38 Special +P with a 110-grain Jacketed Hollow Point (JHP) bullet scores just 1,020 fps and delivers 254 foot pounds of energy. The .357 Magnum with a 110-grain JHP bullet is listed at 1,295 fps and 410 fps.

20.3 Measuring Effectiveness

Calculable kinetic energy is only part of the story. Performance depends upon bullet design. When the 9mm was loaded only with military-type full metal jacketed bullets, it would slice through a target without expending much energy, unless it hit something hard.

In the 1983 *Gun Digest*, Ed Matunas describes his system to evaluate different calibers. He developed a formula to express his *Power Index Rating* (PIR), which retains all the factors used to determine kinetic energy and adds factors for bullet shape, expandability, and caliber.

On his scale, cartridges of less than 95 PIR are popular but inadequate for police use. The .38 Special 158-grain round nose lead bullet fired from a four-inch barrel rates a PIR 56. Even the 125-grain JHP rates only a 79.

Loads rating from 95 to 150, he says, are adequate for police use. This group includes the .38 Special +P 125-grain JHP when fired from a six-inch barrel (PIR 101), but not from a four-inch barrel (PIR 92).

Loads rating 151 or more are effective. This includes the popular .357 Magnum, 125-grain JHP (PIR 177) from a four-inch barrel. But those in the upper range may be hard to control. Any load rating more than 200 is overkill. On this scale, the 9mm, 115-grain JHP rates 129; better than the best .38 Special, but not quite up to the .357 Magnum. With the auto action absorbing some of the recoil, the gun is quite controllable.

Nowadays, the 9mm bullet is designed to react much like similar bullets loaded in either .38 Special or .357 Magnum. This controlled expansion bullet is designed to upset and stop within the target, releasing all of its kinetic energy. This is as true for the 9mm as it is for the popular police revolver calibers.

Having more rounds available, expendable in a shorter time than with a revolver, could make a big difference on the street—especially if you're responding to an armored car hijacking, as did those two officers in Nanuet, New York, when terrorists struck. So, if you're facing the challenge of changing old habits and relying on that "puny" little cartridge, you can rest assured that it is as capable or better than what you used to carry—provided you can put it where it needs to go.

21

The Gun Isn't
the Only Response

There is growing sentiment among some firearms instructors that firearms training should not be as specialized as it is. They feel that firearms should be part of a more comprehensive training program. It is important that you understand this because training emphasizes whatever subject is being taught at the moment. You need to put the pieces together straight in your own mind.

With his growing concern over vicarious liability conflicting with increasing assaults on police officers, your chief faces a perplexing problem. Even if an officer never needs to use his sidearm, it's still a good bet that he will spend time in court defending his reaction to a threat.

He's damned if he uses his gun—and dead if he doesn't. Try explaining that to a layman.

21.1 Firearms Overemphasized?

If training emphasizes only firearms, is the officer conditioned to respond to every threat with his firearm? That is the growing concern among instructors who feel they are overemphasizing one aspect of "threat management," while playing no part in teaching intermediate alternatives to deadly force.

Even such an innocuous utensil as a flashlight is not immune from abuse, as the McDuffy case in Miami taught us. A black was literally bludgeoned to death with flashlights used by police effecting an arrest. A flashlight can be an effective personal defense device, provided the police officer has been adequately trained in its proper use. If the officer receives no training, he is as vulnerable as his employer, according to lawyers I've heard speak on the subject.

The baton is a recognized and "acceptable" device for the uniformed officer to use. He is trained in its proper use. But the officer in plain clothes or off duty won't have a baton at hand. He will have an issue sidearm.

21.2 For Personal Defense

Even though there really are some police departments still using black-jacks, or saps, these devices are hardly acceptable as "defensive" weapons. For the same reason, I rule out Yawara sticks and other such martial arts devices capable of inflicting injury.

I do not rule out the expandable steel baton, such as the *Cobra*, manufactured and distributed by Armament Systems and Procedures, Inc., of Appleton, Wisconsin. This is a six-inch "handle" that extends to some 13 inches with a flick of the wrist. Sturdy enough to use as a conventional baton, it is also convenient to carry; an officer is likely to have it with him as an alternative to deadly force.

But the challenge my training sergeant put to me was to find something purely defensive in nature, convenient to carry, easy to learn, unintimidating in appearance, yet highly effective in controlling either a passive resister or an aggressive suspect.

21.3 An Unintimidating Device

John Peters of the *Defensive Tactics Institute* tells the story of an officer who was sued for "brutality" after taking down a particularly boisterous resister. The judge told the officer to bring the weapon he used into court. When the officer appeared, he didn't have anything in his hand and the judge was irritated.

"Where's your weapon?" the judge asked. "Did you bring it as I asked?"

"Yes, I did, your honor," the officer replied.

"Well, let me see it," said the judge, growing impatient.

The officer placed his key ring on the table. It had a six-inch stick on it, with six grooves apparently providing a grip. When the officer assured

East Hartford (Connecticut) police officer Tom Dumas plays the part of an uncooperative motorist, until John Peters applies the *Kubotan*. Dumas quickly complied.

the judge that this indeed was his weapon, the judge used colorful language and threw the case out of court.

This weapon, the *Kubotan*, with keys on one end, doesn't even raise an eyebrow when you fumble with it. The judge obviously did not consider it an intimidating weapon. It's always in your pocket (or tucked into your belt), and it helps you find your keys. A key ring, pure and simple.

But in the hands of a trained officer, the *Kubotan* enables him to control even the strongest linebacker. The assailant who lunges finds himself on the ground, face down, as the officer cuffs his wrists. A passive resister suddenly sits up and presents his wrists for cuffing. A driver who refuses to get out of the car, quickly changes his mind when the *Kubotan* is applied.

Its use requires no manhandling. When you press the *Kubotan* hard against bone, it pinches the sheath that covers all live bone and causes pain — very convincing pain. It usually leaves no mark.

John Peters tells of incidents where the *Kubotan* has saved lives. A subject had been severely beaten with a baton but continued to fight. A backup officer arrived, applied the *Kubotan*, and quickly subdued the subject. Four hospital orderlies couldn't control a wild mental patient, but the officer they called quickly subdued him with the *Kubotan*.

I'm not saying the *Kubotan* is a panacea. But it is another tool, another alternative that could save your life.

21.4 Instructor Training

When the Smith & Wesson Academy scheduled its first Kubotan Instructor Course, I quickly enrolled. This course is two full days with a minimum of lecture and a maximum of practicing the six simple techniques, variations of which can be used to meet virtually any situation:

• The subject reaches to grab your shirt. Clamp the *Kubotan* on his wrist and step back. He willingly goes to the ground.

• The subject begins to walk away, trying to ignore your command. He can't ignore the *Kubotan* that closes the yoke around his wrist. He goes to the ground ready for cuffing.

• You're simply walking a subject in a position of advantage. If he becomes boisterous, he suddenly finds himself on the ground with the *Kubotan* applying a thumblock that makes him eager for handcuffs.

• The subject tries to punch you but is surprised to discover that he has presented you with his wrist. He is quickly on the ground.

• The subject lunges, but his chest meets the *Kubotan*. He spins around, sits, and then flops face down ready for cuffing.

• The subject needs to be frisked, and there's no wall to lean him against. The officer is vulnerable. A *Kubotan* between the outstretched fingers is held by the officer's outside hand while his inside hand pats the subject down. Any resistance is quickly discouraged by pain.

There's much more to the application of *Kubotan* techniques. But secrets needn't be disclosed in print when you must take the course to become certified. One man from your department, sent to a Kubotan Instructor Course, comes back certified to train other officers in the basic course.

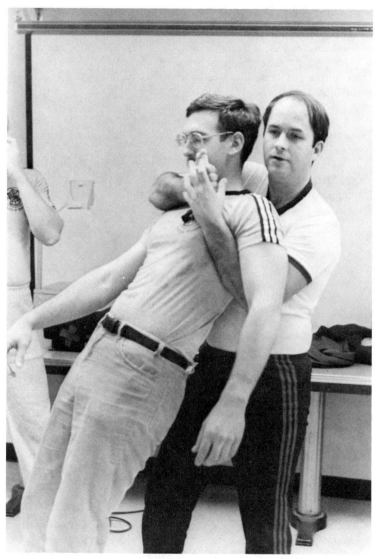

This student in our instructor class was facing Peters until the *Kubotan*, applied in the right spot, spun him around. Downward pressure in the right spot, in front of the shoulder, then put him down into a sitting position—without argument. One hump of the knee, and the "aggressor" ended up face-down with his hands behind his back ready for cuffing.

21.5 Certification Is Important

Training must be based on specific criteria developed through definitive research, and it must prescribe a course of study. Generally, certification by a recognized training institution — such as the S&W Academy and Kubotan Institute — is defensible in court. It shows the judge that the department's instructor has been deemed competent to train others and to certify you as competent to apply the techniques taught.

It means that you don't stand alone in court when you have to qualify the training program and justify your actions. Recognized certification may even discourage litigation.

True, it may never go beyond your presenting your "key ring" to the judge. Yet it may avoid the necessity of reaching for your hip when the situation falls short of the opportunity, capability, and threat criteria that justifies the use of deadly force.

22

Making the Big Decision

Firearms training, now more than ever, includes the consideration of whether to shoot or not to shoot. Realistic targets force you to decide, then take proper action. "Shoot–Don't Shoot" films point out the problems of making that big decision.

When you pull the trigger, three criteria must be met: capability, opportunity, and jeopardy.

A simple example: The man walking out of the sporting goods store with a baseball bat has the capability, but you don't shoot. When he turns in your direction and comes within a few feet of you he has the opportunity, but you don't shoot. When he raises the bat to take a swing at your head, he places you in jeopardy. Then you shoot.

Even if your state has the "fleeing felon" law, there is judicial precedence that you cannot apply in all cases. The kid running from a stolen car, for example, may be a fleeing felon; but he fails to meet any of the criteria above.

The thinking today is leaning toward a more restrictive policy that may prevent legislators from wanting to change the law. You should be aware of what police chiefs are thinking. As a member of the Firearms Committee of the Connecticut Police Chiefs Association, we adopted in our state the model policy of the *International Association of Chiefs of Police*. With additional modifications for generic application, the following represents what may soon be imposed on you, if it hasn't been already:

Model Deadly Force Policy
Definition

The term "deadly force," as used in this policy, is defined as that force, by whatever means imposed, which is likely to cause death or grave injury, or which creates some specified degree of risk that a reasonable and prudent person would consider likely to cause death or grave injury.

Disclaimer

This policy standard is intended for departmental use only, and does not apply in any criminal or civil proceeding. The policy should not be construed as the creation of a higher standard of safety or care in an evidentiary sense with respect to third party claims. Violations of law will form the basis for civil and criminal sanctions in a recognized court having jurisdiction.

Protection of Life

The value of human life in our society is immeasurable. Police officers are charged with the awesome responsibility to protect life and property, and to apprehend criminal offenders. The apprehension of criminal offenders and the protection of property must be subservient to the protection of life. The police officer's responsibility for protecting life must include his own.

A police officer may use deadly force to protect himself or others from what he reasonably believes to be an immediate threat of death, or critical bodily harm. He may also use deadly force to effect the capture, or prevent the escape of a suspect whose freedom is reasonably believed to represent a threat of death or grave bodily harm to others. Self-defense and perceived threats of death or grave bodily harm shall be the only considerations for employing the use of deadly force.

Use of Firearms

By the definition above, deadly force can be inflicted by a variety of instruments; but the one specific to police is the firearm. Therefore, protection of life and self-defense policies notwithstanding, the following are recommended guidelines concerning the use of firearms by police officers:

1. Police officers should not discharge firearms when it appears likely that an innocent person may be killed or injured.

2. Police officers should not discharge firearms at or from a moving vehicle, except as the ultimate measure of self-defense or defense of another when a suspect is using deadly force from a vehicle by any means including the vehicle itself.

3. Police officers should not use a firearm to fire a "warning" shot.

4. The shooting of an animal by a police officer is justified only (a.) for self-defense, (b.) to prevent serious or substantial harm to the officer or another person, and (c.) for humane purposes as may be provided by state law or town ordinance.

Firearms Training and Standards

All on-duty officers should be armed with a department-approved firearm loaded with department-approved ammunition. There should be a department standard for type and caliber of handgun and appropriate ammunition with bullet weight and design specified. All other department firearms and ammunition should be classified as special purpose weapons.

A secondary (or backup) on-duty handgun should be authorized with written authorization by the Chief.

Police officers should be encouraged to carry a handgun when off duty, but should exercise discretion where being armed is inappropriate. An officer unarmed and off duty shall not be subject to disciplinary action if an occasion should arise in which he could have taken police action if he were armed.

A department-approved handgun (on duty, backup, or off duty) intended for official use by a police officer should meet the following requirements:

1. The standard firearm should be not less than .38 caliber.

2. The firearm should be loaded only with department-approved ammunition with bullet weight and design specified; controlled expansion bullets are recommended.

3. The firearm should be inspected, fired, and certified safe by a department armorer or range officer.

4. The firearm should be registered with the department by make, model, caliber, and serial number.

5. An officer should demonstrate safe and proficient use of each approved firearm during regular firearms qualification sessions.

6. An officer should meet "certification" requirements with each type of weapon he is authorized to carry.

All officers shall be "certified" with their primary and secondary on-duty firearms and any approved off-duty firearms. "Certification" shall include formal training regarding the legal, moral, and ethical aspects of firearms use; safety in the handling of firearms; and proficiency in the use of firearms.

Firearms "certification" shall be required at least quarterly, consisting of a minimum of sixteen (16) hours per year. And, in the event of any accidental discharge of a firearm, the officer involved must undergo immediate re-certification training.

Post-Shooting Investigation and Inquiry

Written departmental procedures should be established and used to investigate *every* incident of firearms discharge by a department member, except for firearms training, hunting, ballistic examinations, and incidents involving the justified destruction of an animal.

Such departmental orders must define, as a minimum, the responsibilities of the following:

1. *Uniformed Patrol Commander*; to assist involved officers and conduct a preliminary on-site field investigation.

2. *Criminal Investigation Unit*; to conduct a complete and thorough investigation to determine all relevant facts.

3. *Internal Affairs Unit*; to conduct an internal investigation — subordinate to any criminal investigation — to determine whether the shooting conformed to established policy or was accidental.

4. *Shooting Committee or Board*; appointed by the Chief to review the established facts and circumstances attendant to each discharge of a firearm by a department member. This group should develop findings and make any appropriate recommendations to the Chief.

If I had to come up with a simple statement, I'd put it this way:

"Your honor, I reasonably believed, based on my experience, that it was the only way I could *stop the perpetrator's felonious action* that placed myself or someone else at risk of death or serious injury."

Remember the underlined phrase. That's the *only* reason you ever pull the trigger.

(Continued from front flap)

BILL CLEDE has over 30 years of experience in police work and as a writer-photographer. His police duties cover the gamut from traffic duty to training other police officers in advanced-firearms know-how at the Smith & Wesson Academy. He has worked for major firearms companies and is a Life Member of the National Rifle Association. Clede, who lives in Connecticut, is widely known for his syndicated column in police publications.